CHOOSE YOUR LIFE

Living The Abundant Life

By Tiery Phanor

Unless otherwise indicated, all Scripture quotations are taken from the New Living Translation version of the Bible.

All Scripture quotations marked NKJV are taken from the New King James version of the Bible.

All Scripture quotations marked KJV are taken from the King James version of the Bible.

CHOOSE LIFE
ISBN-13:
978-0615894140

ISBN-10:
0615894143

Dedication

This book is dedicated to my lovely wife, Tonia, the woman of my dreams, my counselor, my partner, and my best friend, without her, the release of this great venture would not be possible. You amaze me more every day, and you are the greatest gift God could have ever given me. Thank you princess!

To Kayann J Phanor and Arthur J Phanor, my two precious children, you give me the strength to keep going whenever I feel like to giving up on my dreams.

To my mother Marie Pauline Augustin, who raised six children as a single mother when my father passed away when I was seven years old. You are the description of a strong Black woman. Thank you for raising me to be the man I am today. To my mother in-law Ruth East, thank you for accepting me as your son, your daily prayers and support mean the world to me.

To my siblings: Walker Phanor, Alma Phanor, Adrienne Phanor, Phara Phanor , and Kendler Phanor; I love you all very much.

Finally, to all my those who have despised, rejected, talked about me, and misunderstood my calling. I would have not sought intensely after God's will for my life through prayer and fasting. If it were not for these hurts and pains, I would not be the man I am today. These people have played a big role in my life also, thank you.

Acknowledgments

As with any major venture, it takes a great team of people to make all the essentials come together in a book.

To Claude Pierre, thank you for being my brother in Christ, and one of the first people to support this book.

Thank you to my editors, Betty Chaney, Tonia Phanor, and Dawn Washington. I cannot thank you enough for the work you put in to make this book what it is today.

Thank you to all my supporters and encouragers. Mrs. Nativita Joseph, your love for me blesses me every day. You are my cousin, my sister, my prayer warrior. To Mr. Guercy Joseph, thank you for your prayers and example. To Ms. Carole Jerome, you make me feel that I could conquer the world even when I did not believe in myself. To Dr. Mireille Michel Simon, your godly knowledge and exceptional insights have made me stronger every day. Last, but not least, to all the mighty men and women of Revelation of Church, your love and support had kept me going forward from many trials.

Table of Contents

Introduction.. 7

1 Intimacy with God 9

2 The Wilderness Experience................... 23

3 Embrace the Vision........................... 39

4 Selecting a Spouse........................... 51

5 Let's Talk About Sex! 69

6 Escape from Temptation...................... 81

7 Forgiveness................................... 93

8 Trusting God................................ 107

9 The Love of God.......................... 121

10 The Privilege of Holiness................. 129

INTRODUCTION

Broken. Wounded. Undone. God originally ordained me to write this book in a very difficult season of my lifetime. Hardship often leaves us with many spoken and unspoken questions before God. It is difficult for the believer to comprehend that God would allow His people to face terrible situations, such as unemployment, divorce, or loss of loved ones. How can a great God allow such terrible things to come to pass? Didn't He declare in His that He came that we might have 'life' and that 'more abundantly?'

It is difficult to appreciate God's promises when we don't understand His process. In order for us to receive the promises of God, we must understand His will for us. Looking back, I can see how God used trials (*not triumphs*) to strengthen my faith, my study of His , and my ministry. God's goal was to get to the end of me that His will might be accomplished *through* me.

As you journey through this book, my prayer is that God will unveil to you crucial decisions in key areas of your life that are necessary to living abundantly. It is far more than houses and fine cars. God wants so much more... He desires to penetrate every aspect of your life. As a matter of fact, He sent His Son so that you could *have* life. No matter where you are in your spiritual walk, I want to challenge you to take a moment to evaluate your life. From the pulpit to the pews, God desires that each and every one of us live abundantly in Him. If you will lend me your ear, I will share the things God has revealed to me along this road.

CHAPTER ONE
INTIMACY WITH GOD

Intimacy is a term often associated with romantic relationships, cozy settings and candle-lit bedrooms. When we spend time with an individual, we begin to understand the individual's perspective, and the individual's personality, or what that individual values most in his or her life, even the personal life of the person. However, when we think of our relationship with God, it is challenging for our finite minds to comprehend a close relationship with an infinite God. Let's take a moment and ponder what it means to be intimate with God. In the context of this book, I would like to define intimacy as the experience of becoming a friend of God by knowing His character, His lifestyle and His personality. It is almost impossible to reflect Christ if we have never taken the time to get to know Him in a personal experience and become familiar with his characteristics. Many people claim they want to know God, but they never take the time to fellowship with Him. In order for us to get to know Him or resemble Him, we must understand that we were created to fulfill God's purpose.

The Apostle Paul shares his heart to the churches at Philippi:

"But what things were gain to me, those I counted loss for Christ. Yea doubtless, and I count all things but loss for the excellency of the knowledge of Christ Jesus my Lord: for whom I have suffered the loss of all things, and do count them but dung, that I may win Christ, And be found in him, not having mine own righteousness, which is of the law, but that which is through the faith of Christ, the righteousness which is of God by faith: That I may know him, and the power of his resurrection, and the fellowship of his sufferings, being made conformable unto his death;" Philippians 3:7-10 (KJV)

This intimate friendship is birthed first from God being our Father and Christ being God the 'Son.' Before Adam sinned, he had a relationship with God. When he disobeyed God, he lost the privilege of being in a relationship with the Lord our God. Since Adam could not fully fulfill the will of God, Jesus Christ came to accomplish everything Adam could not fulfill. Jesus, the Son of God, brought us a second time into relationship with His Father when He died a criminal's death on the cross. Our carnal minds were disconnected from God. As a result, God had to find a way to bring us back into relationship with Him once more, so He could destroy our carnal mindset, which we inherited from our first father Adam. Therefore, we have a second chance to fellowship with our heavenly Father for a lifetime. All we must do is thank Christ for paying the penalty for our sin and ask Him to forgive us and take over as our Lord and Savior. Let us not take His suffering for granted but rather seek to 'know Him' intimately.

God is looking for people who will take the time to communicate with Him, so He can share His plan for humanity. When we seek God's will and acknowledge Him in our daily activities, He will reveal His personality and His purposes for our lives. God's desire is to let everyone know *plainly* about his or her purpose. As we become conscious of His plan for our lives, we will be diligent in keeping a daily communication with our Lord Jesus Christ.

An intimate life with Christ is a choice. Chapter after chapter, I will permeate these pages with one idea… choice. Individual responsibility. The life you live before our most holy God is a choice you make. Choose life!

PRESSURE PRODUCED INTIMACY

Jesus tells the disciples in John 16:33 (KJV), "These things I have spoken unto you, that in me ye might have peace. In the world *ye shall have tribulation*: but be of good cheer; I have overcome the world." Dear believer, one thing is for sure and two for certain, we will face trials and hardship. God's intention is to strengthen believers as He allows us to experience some hardships: it is an opportunity for us to develop spiritual muscle, so we can be able to grow stronger in our faith.

When we encounter difficulties, we tend to look to God for answers. It is in these times that we begin to pray more or seek the presence of God. Some may begin to worship more, singing songs of praise, and becoming convinced that God has answered their prayers. We need to comprehend that God's desires to make us like His Son, Jesus Christ, who put His complete faith and trust in God. When Jesus Christ came to the earth, He was here to do the will of the Father, not His own will. Therefore, we must be willing to **pursue** the example of His Son, Jesus Christ. When we live our lives the way we want and not the way God requires of us to live, it indicates that we do not belong to Him. A son who loves his father will revere his father with obedience. If we say that we love God, we will do whatever it takes to obey His instructions. A son is willing to do this because of a relationship founded upon trust in his father.

One of the most important things every believer needs to understand is that in *every relationship there must be some degree of trust*. This trust must take place before individuals can fearlessly feel comfortable trusting one another with their hearts or their possessions. It is time for *us*, believers, to trust God with all of our hearts and stop wavering in our faith, so the power of the Holy Spirit can exercise on earth. Consequently, He creates strategies to cause us to trust Him… draw us closer to Him by allowing us to face some type of hardships or calamities. God will do whatever He thinks necessary to bring His children into relationship with Him.

When we face difficulties in life, it means that God is burning everything in us, which does not belong to Him. God's intention is to demonstrate to the world that Jesus Christ is still walking among us. Therefore, people will perceive Christ through us, His believers. In order to share this level of intimacy with God, we must trust that He is not out to harm us but rather to help us. What a beautiful thing for us believers to know that Jesus Christ loves us more than anything we can ever imagine. John 3:16 (KJV) declares, "For God so loved the world that He gave His only begotten Son that whosoever believes in Him will not perish but have eternal life.

When God allows believers to go through some difficult moments in life, let it be an opportunity for us to grow spiritually. When a father wants his children to grow in a certain area of life, he will allow them to experience difficult times. Consequently, that child will develop some level of maturity. Therefore, do not let Satan make you believe that God does not care for His children, because He had allowed us to go through a difficult situation. He uses our hurts to heal us. He uses the dry places to make us thirsty for Him. He covers us with his love in our loneliness. He uses our failures to build our faith.

PRAYER PRODUCED INTIMACY

As citizens of Heaven, we must continue to stay in daily communication with our King, so we can do whatever He desires for us to do on earth. Now, how can we live at this level communion? When Jesus Christ came on earth, He spent most of his life seeking the will of His Father. Even though He already clearly knew what the will of God was for His life, He wanted to make sure that He had developed a daily communication with Him through prayer and fasting. Jesus understood it would be almost impossible to do the will of God without Him living a prayerful lifestyle.

I have realized that the body of Christ has become powerless because our leaders and laity alike have desired the things of this world more than the things of God: things such as the number of members attending their church every Sunday, fancy cars and raising large offerings. Instead of them seeking the heart of God, they are more concerned about earthly things. Sinning with no regard is a byproduct of a lack of prayerful intimacy with God. The body of Christ needs to do its best and learn to operate as the children of God.

In this era, it is time to get serious about getting closer to God. In the church today, we have pastors, evangelists, and Sunday school teachers, who spend month after month in church, yet never take the time to pray or fast because they were, too busy preaching the gospel. Too often, we live a hectic lifestyle because of the things of this world; as a result, we have failed to spend enough time with our Lord. I believe this is the reason why it has become so difficult for believers to understand the will of God for their lives. Personal intimacy *with* God must be a priority before public service *to* God.

When our Lord Jesus Christ was here on earth, He prayed, fasted, and sought the will of His Father because He wanted to connect with him. He was both man and God, yet He spent most of his time praying to God the Father. We need to take notice of what we carry on the inside of us; as a result, we'll have the opportunity to minister with power to others. Remember, we do not belong to this world; we are ambassadors of Christ, and therefore, we must value our assignments because two thousand years ago Jesus came into this world to carry out the assignments, which the Father had granted Him. Keep in mind that our assignment begins the day we accept Christ. Therefore, we must reprioritize our focus. As a result, we will have the mind of Christ.

One final note on prayer… God is hungry to see His children spend quality time with Him in prayer. He longs for us to learn how to pray according to what the Holy Spirit has been revealing to us. When we pray according to the will of God, we do not have to ask Him to bless what we pray for because we will automatically experience His blessing…it's HIS WILL being done. When God designs a specific thing for His children to do, it is because He has already predestined us to carry out that assignment. God's tangible presence in a Christian's life is the most essential thing we should long for in our daily prayer. When we are in the presence of our King, He will cause everything, which is not working in our lives, to work perfectly.

PRESENCE OF HIS SPIRIT IN MEDITATION PRODUCES INTIMACY

How do we become one in mind with Christ? For us to have the mind of Christ, we first need to spend most of our time in His and meditating in his Holy presence. Many people want to be intimate with God, but only a few are willing to take the time to get to know Him. When we make a decision to seek after the heart of God, we will begin to display His love in our lives. Consequently, we will become more like Him. His power will begin to manifest in our daily lives and ministries, and people will long after what we carry inside of us. Jesus said, "the things I do shall you do, even greater things shall you do." However, it is impossible to display the power of the Holy Spirit without *intimacy with God* because the Holy Spirit is the mediator, who connects us Christians to God and Jesus.

The Holy Spirit is the mediator that brings men and God into relationships. In other words, if we do not have the Holy Spirit, it is impossible to be intimate with God. Jesus called the Holy Spirit the counselor. A counselor is someone who mentors a person or comforts a person. Thus, when we have the Holy Spirit, we will automatically sense the presence of God in our lives, as we begin to devote ourselves to His mission, and dedicating our lives to His way of doing things. When we allow Him to be the center of our lives, He will begin to direct our paths. Whenever we go astray, He will show us the proper way to go. I can attest that my life is powerless without the help of the Holy Spirit.

If you are a believer and you are reading this book, ask yourself this question. Do I have a close relationship with God? If you do not, you are just hurting yourself. God is the source of every Christian. We decide to separate ourselves from the presence of God by not spending enough time with Him, and then we begin a church without even having a relationship with Him for ourselves. This is the reason why some ministers have become depressed because they are performing a task for which they were not *empowered* by the presence of God to do. It is imperative that we stay close to God, so He can pour His love and His strength in us *before* we can start pouring ourselves into someone else's life.

When we spend time in the presence of our Lord Jesus, it becomes much easier for us to perform any ministerial gift, which He has entrusted to us. Being intimate with God is the key for spiritual empowerment in our ministry, as it enables us to fulfill the plan of God for our lives. Many want God's blessings, but only a few are willing to follow His way and His principles. There was a young man in the Bible who asked Jesus a very important question:

"Jesus, how can I enter into the system of heaven?" He asked.

"You must first give away everything you have then follow me," Jesus said.

Nevertheless, the young man thought Jesus was trying to get something from Him, instead of blessing Him. Jesus was trying to help Him make an investment that would last for a lifetime; I assume believers react the same way. Whenever God requires of us to do something for Him or let go of something, it is because He wants to bring us closer to Him, or empower us in a certain area. However, we tend to react as if we know better than God does. As a result, we settle and go our own way because we do not understand His plan. God never said being a Christian was going to be an easy commission, but He did say, we must deny ourselves, take up our cross and follow Him.

We should always keep in mind that the Holy Spirit is an instrument to empower believers, so we can accomplish the will of God, not our own. The problem is that there are people who seek God only for what He can do for them, so they don't really have the desire to be in His presence. They fail to realize that the empowerment of the Holy Spirit came at a great cost. When we fail to understand what He went through in order to save us sinners, and when we take His crucifixion for granted, we are actually crucifying Him for a second time. Therefore, we must never take His sacrifice for granted; the Bible states how God created

Christ, who knew no sin, to be sin for us that we might become the righteousness of God (II Cor. 5:21). What a beautiful thing for us to know that Jesus Christ loves us more than anything we can ever imagine. God so loved the world that He gave His only begotten Son whoever believes in Him will not perish but have eternal life (John 3:16). Furthermore, we know have access to His holy presence through the Holy Spirit.

PRAISE PRODUCES INTIMACY

One of the most essential tools we fail to utilize in Christianity is the gift of worship. Worship is the most powerful tool that can bring us closer to God. When we take the time to worship God and sing praise songs to Him, we demonstrate that we are truly seeking His heart. We must realize nothing pleases our Lord and Savior more than to have His children worshipping Him and glorifying His name. Worship is the heart of God. The scripture tells us that there are angelic beings worshiping God at all times in the heavenly realm. He wants to consume our worship as we minister to Him through songs and music. Therefore, it is clear that our Father is hungry for our worship. Let us make a decision to spend enough time in His holy presence, so we can continue to please Him through our worships and praises.

Often time as a pastor, I visit diverse churches. Discontent consumes me by the manner in which some church leaders conduct the services. They put a time limit about how long each service should last. For example, when the Spirit of God begins to move through a song or a certain melody, but because they have put a time limit in the length of the service, they hinder the very presence of the Holy Spirit to move through the service. It should never be the order of the service, instead the order of the Holy Spirit. God's desire is **not** for us to stop the Holy Spirit, as He begins to manifest Himself in a worship service.

As we take the time to fellowship with our Father and contemplate in His holy presence, He will answer our prayers, and whenever we call upon Him, He will deliver us from our afflictions. When we remain in the presence of God, we have confirmed that He is our only source. It is in the exclusivity of worship… intimacy is nurtured. We must worship God at all cost. Nothing is more important than our time spent with Him. I'll close this chapter with a true story from sacred scripture.

> Six days before the Passover, Jesus therefore came to Bethany, where Lazarus was, whom Jesus had raised from the dead. So they gave a dinner for him there. Martha served, and Lazarus was one of those reclining with him at table. Mary therefore took a pound of expensive ointment made from pure nard, and anointed the feet of Jesus and wiped his feet with her hair. The house was filled with the fragrance of the perfume. But Judas Iscariot, one of his disciples (he who was about to betray

him), said, "Why was this ointment not sold for three hundred denarii and given to the poor?" He said this, not because he cared about the poor, but because he was a thief, and having charge of the moneybag he used to help himself to what was put into it. Jesus said, "Leave her alone, so that she may keep it for the day of my burial. For the poor you always have with you, but you do not always have me." John 12:1-8 (ESV)

As the woman with the alabaster box of precious perfume, we must appreciate the privilege of being in the presence of God. We must not wait until we encounter difficulties to pray, worship, or seek the presence of the Holy Spirit. As believers, we must realize that it is God's intention for us to be in constant fellowship with Him as His Son, Jesus Christ, stayed in communion with the Father. Intimacy with God must be privately pursued and publically displayed that the world might know who Jesus Christ is! In Him is life... Choose Life!

CHAPTER TWO
THE WILDERNESS EXPERIENCE

Being in the wilderness can be a very uncomfortable place for believers to find themselves and can bring many questions into our minds. *"Why am I here, God?" "Have you forsaken me?" "Why does this hurt so bad?" "When will it end?"* Whenever troubles take place in our lives instead of asking God what is His plan in the difficulty that we face, we want to get out of the problem without understanding its purpose. Every problem has purpose. The wilderness is a place that believers need to embrace instead of running away from it. It can be the most joyful and/or painful moment we ever experience in our lives. The wilderness is where the children of God develop character, trust, patience, spiritual maturity, and dependence on God. When we obey God in the wilderness by allowing Him to be the center of our lives, it becomes the most joyful event. However, when we refuse to follow the will of God in the wilderness, it becomes a most painful place. What we need to ask ourselves is why we go through it?

THE PURPOSE OF THE WILDERNESS: PREPARATION

The main purpose for the wilderness is to bring us in accordance with the perfect will of God, so He can prepare us for his divine plan. It is designed to *prepare* us for our mission. The wilderness is a necessary certification examination for believers in order to validate them as true citizens of the Kingdom. When we face difficult situations, God is developing godly character in us while simultaneously preparing us for a specific task. When God called Moses to bring the children of Israel out of Egypt from slavery, God never said it was going to be a painless experience for them. He wanted them to learn to trust Him, and to put their complete faith in Him. One of the biggest mistakes believers make is that every time we encounter difficulty instead of embracing the challenge, we look for a way to escape from the circumstances that God has purposely designed for us.

Let us take a moment to analyze God's intention for the children of Israel in the wilderness. As we begin to read the Book of Exodus, we could clearly see that the children of Israel did not know God's ability. They had not learned to depend on Him for Pharaoh was their supplier, and everything they needed came from Pharaoh's hands. As a result, God had to teach them about the God of their ancestors: Abraham, Isaac, and Jacob. God was willing to be a provider for them, but He allowed them to experience some level of hardship, so they could witness the power of God in their lives. So, when the children of Israel left Egypt, Moses took them to a bizarre place that did not make much sense to their natural minds. It was a place where there was no other alternative. The Egyptian Army was chasing them to destroy them, while they stood in front of the Red

Sea with nowhere to go. Follow me to the scene in
Exodus 14...

Now the Lord spoke to Moses, saying: "Speak
to the children of Israel, that they turn and camp
before Pi Hahiroth, between Migdol and the sea,
opposite Baal Zephon; you shall camp before it
by the sea. For Pharaoh will say of the children
of Israel, 'They are bewildered by the land; the
wilderness has closed them in.' Then I will
harden Pharaoh's heart, so that he will pursue
them; and I will gain honor over Pharaoh and
over all his army, that the Egyptians may know
that I am the Lord." And they did so. Now it
was told the king of Egypt that the people had
fled, and the heart of Pharaoh and his servants
was turned against the people; and they said,
"Why have we done this, that we have let Israel
go from serving us?"..... For it would have
been better for us to serve the Egyptians than
that we should die in the wilderness." And
Moses said to the people, *"Do not be afraid.
Stand still, and see the salvation of the Lord,
which He will accomplish for you today. For
the Egyptians whom you see today, you shall
see again no more forever. The Lord will fight
for you, and you shall hold your peace."* And
the Lord said to Moses, "Why do you cry to
Me? **Tell the children of Israel to go forward.**
But lift up your rod, and stretch out your hand
over the sea and divide it. And the children of
Israel shall go on dry ground through the midst

of the sea. And I indeed will harden the hearts of the Egyptians, and they shall follow them. So I will gain honor over Pharaoh and over all his army, his chariots, and his horsemen. Then the Egyptians shall know that I am the Lord, when I have gained honor for Myself over Pharaoh, his chariots, and his horsemen." Exodus 14:1-18 (NKJV, emphasis mine)

God didn't panic at the tremendous obstacles the children of Israel had before them because he already knew what he would do. It could be argued that God brought them in that place because He wanted them to have their eyes focused on Him not on the Red Sea, and to reveal His ability to them. He was their God and their provider in time of need. He had to bring them to an impossible situation, by bringing them to the Red Sea they could experience the power of God to make a way out of no way.

Sometimes troubles will occur because God wants to prepare us for a bigger trial that is going to take place in the future. Therefore, He allows something to happen, so He can perform miracles to build up our trust in Him. In other words, the Israelites did not really grasp the plan of God for their lives. Consequently, He had to allow them to go through a process of faith development, so He could help them develop some level of self-assurance. The wilderness is not there to destroy us, but it is designed to build us up for greater responsibilities, and for the opportunities that God has in store for us. The body of Christ needs to renew its mind with the Word of God, and to understand that adversities only come to those whom God can trust and those whom He's preparing. If you are in the worst moment of your life, you need to rejoice and be glad in the Lord because God is getting ready to promote you. As a result, you can get to the next dimension in life. We must remember God's love is greater than any affliction or problem we can ever experience.

PRAYER IN THE WILDERNESS

Prayer is essential in our wilderness experiences. When we go through our wilderness, we need to learn *how to* pray by faith. Too often we pray *against* the very situation that is tailor made for us by the will of God for our lives. God has not left us without an instructor. Since we do not understand what God has planned, we need to acknowledge the help of the Holy Spirit. According to Romans 8, the Holy Spirit is an intimate factor is our prayer life. He is there to show us how to pray in accordance with God's will. Listen to the words of the Apostle Paul...

> *Likewise the Spirit also helps in our weaknesses. For we do not know what we should pray for as we ought, but the Spirit Himself makes intercession for us with groanings which cannot be uttered. Now He who searches the hearts knows what the mind of the Spirit is, because He makes intercession for the saints according to the will of God.* Romans 8:26-27 (NKJV)

When we fail to pray according to the will of God in our difficulties, we end up delaying the process of conquering our promise land. When God gives a dream or a vision to His children, He often doesn't elaborate on how everything is going to take place. However, He constantly challenges us to trust Him no matter what the circumstances are. When things are not going the way we desire, we need to ask ourselves if we are in the perfect will of God. If we are in the will of God, everything is going to ultimately work out for our good (Romans 8:28). Beloved, understand God's will is not an easy thing to fulfill. Sometimes, God can allow us to go through some things in life that our pastors, our spiritual fathers or our spouses, who are the closest individuals in our lives, may not understand or have the answers. However, we must carry our cross daily and follow Jesus. The cross represents the Christian lifestyle: the pains and suffering that Christians must undergo, the flesh that needs to be crucified, the humility of life, the headaches, the pains of this world, and the temptation we must resist on a daily basis. We must endure so we can inherit the gift of eternal life, which Jesus Christ paid for us on Calvary. He gave up everything for our sake, so we can have access to the throne of God.

PROBLEMS IN THE WILDERNESS

When we want to achieve a dream, we must be determined to make sacrifices in order to achieve that dream. The crisis that most people have to deal with is visualizing in the natural what God has foreordained in the spiritual realm. When God was creating the universe, He called it into existence; in other words, whatever existed in the spiritual realm, God called it out into existence in the natural realm. There are no surprises for God, and everything that He allows to happen is under His control. In Jeremiah 1:5, the Lord said to Jeremiah, *"I knew you before I formed you in your mother's womb. Before you were born I set you apart and appointed you to be my spokesman to the world."* Jeremiah existed in the spiritual realm; his spirit was created to be a spokesperson for God long ago, but Jeremiah did not understand that God had created him to be a spokesperson for Him. Nevertheless, Jeremiah had to endure several trials and tribulations in order for him to adjust to who he was in the spiritual realm.

Whenever we encounter trials and tribulations, God is shaping our flesh to come into agreement with our spirit. Our spirits were already born to be in agreement with God before our bodies took on flesh. Consequently, our spirit will automatically submit to the plans of God, because our spirit came from God. In contrast, our flesh came from Adam. This is why God will put us into hard situations to shape us to agree with His plans, so we can do what we were called to do. Every time we get up in the morning, God is looking for ways, and strategies to make us take notice of His purpose, which He wants us to accomplish here on earth. If we take the time to listen to His voice, then we will understand why we are going through these situations. They are only here to prepare us for greatness. Sometimes, we please people more than we please God; perhaps God is asking you to do some thing or go somewhere, which does not make a lot of sense to your friends or family members, so instead of obeying the voices of God, you begin reasoning with God, and thus despising His instructions.

If God clearly speaks to you about a specific task that He wills for you to accomplish, do not debate it with anyone. Just go and do exactly what God tells you to do! For example, some of us are in a relationship with someone that we know is not the will of God for us. However, since we cannot control our emotions, we would rather disobey God and live a rebellious life. Whenever God commands His children to do something, and we do not obey Him, His hands of discipline will be heavy against us. Discipline often follows us on the paths of distraction.

The best weapon Satan uses against the body Christ is distraction, or making propositions that are not according to God's Word. However, if we truly understand the Word of God, and are determined to live by it, we will be able to conquer the enemy's deception. Satan will always try to ambush believers. When we are experiencing the weakest moment of our lives, or when we are going to perform something significant for the Kingdom of God, that is when Satan will try to discourage us the most. Jesus, after fasting for forty days, and forty nights, the Bible said that He ate nothing, and He was very hungry. Then Satan took the opportunity to tempt Jesus while He was facing the greatest hunger in His lifetime. Satan also understood that Jesus was about to fulfill what God had preordained in His public ministry.

The body of Christ needs to remember that we have a daily battle to fight against the devil; he will use whatever he can to make us believe our situation will last forever. Christians will be tested, but when our faith is tested, let it be an opportunity for us to rejoice because God only lets those whom He can trust be tested. He knew they would not disappoint him. Therefore, if God allowed trouble to come your way, you need to stay encouraged, because breakthrough is on the way. We should never let Satan take notice of our weaknesses; if you are a born again believer and filled with the Spirit of God; Satan cannot control your mind nor make you do anything you do not want to do. The only weapon he could use against us is to make us propositions. Consider Genesis...

Genesis 3:1-5 (NLT) states, *"Now the serpent was the shrewdest of all the creatures the Lord had made. Did God really say you must not eat any of the fruit in the garden?" "Of course we may eat it," Eve told him. "It's only the fruit from the tree of the center of the garden that we are not allowed to eat. God says we must not eat or even touch it, or we will die." "You won't die," the serpent hissed. "God knows your eyes will be opened when you eat it. You will become just like God, knowing everything both good and evil." He said.*

As we notice, Satan did not put any pressure on the woman to disobey God and to eat the fruit; however, he played with her mind, and advised her to eat the fruit, which she was not supposed to eat. Satan will always twist the truth. The body of Christ needs to have the zeal to always obey God, even though it may be a very difficult thing to do. Nevertheless, those who obey God will always be rewarded. When we allow ourselves to be governed by the Spirit of God instead of the flesh, we will always live a victorious life.

PRACTICAL APPLICATION IS LEARNED IN THE WILDERNESS

A while ago, I was a guest speaker at a church. At the end of the service, I talked with a good friend of mine, who told me that she would leave her church of eleven years because there was a big conflict between her and the Pastor of the church. I told her, if God puts it in your heart to leave the church, you should do it, but do not leave the church without an instruction from God. On many occasions, people make decisions without even consulting their leaders. We end up finding ourselves in miserable places. Remember when God has assigned you to a church, or put you under a specific ministry, it is because you are a big part of that particular ministry. We cannot allow our emotions or weaknesses to push us away from the will of God for our lives. Sometimes, God stretches our faith, and patience, so we can develop self-control, and spiritual fruit that will last for a lifetime. Every time God appoints a man or a woman to fulfill a certain task, He always sends an impossible predicament, so He can show His ability to them. Our afflictions are beneficial for us believers. What we need to do is to embrace every trial that He allows us to go through.

I encourage every believer never to take for granted the disappointments and the hurts, which we encounter in life. When I woke up one morning, I took my then four-year-old son to school. After I dropped him off to school, I stopped at a park to talk to God about some financial difficulties that I was dealing with. I asked the Lord to speak to me because I did not know what to do. After the prayer, I left the park and went home. When I got to the gate, I saw a sign that said, "God has everything under control." It was very astonishing because I had been living at that apartment complex for over two years, and I had never noticed that sign before, God knows where we are in life, and He will never leave us nor forsake us.

I understand sometimes God can tell us to do something significant, but when we look at our current positions in life, it does not seem like it's going to happen. However, this is when we need to believe God even more. Friends, this is the time we need to press on more toward the dream, and the vision that God puts in our hearts. When, we find ourselves in a very intense situation, it means we are closer to giving birth to our dream. When a woman is pregnant, during the first seven months of her pregnancy, she may be able to perform her daily tasks with no complications.

However, when she is getting ready to give birth, she begins to experience very intense pains. God has a plan for every believer, but the reason why it seems so hard for us to understand His plan is that our minds are not yet renewed by His Word. When we begin to dig into the Word of God, we will understand why our trials are not here to destroy us but instead to strengthen our faith.

Every time, we as believers, take a stand to do God's will even when we have to face persecutions in life, the blessing of God will continue to flow in our lives. On November 31, 2009, I faced a very complex dilemma. God had instructed me to start a church. Six months after I opened the church, my job told me that I must work on Sundays. I had to make a decision: would I continue with the vision that God had given me, or would I relinquish my employment. I resigned from my position and continued with the plan of God for my life. When I looked at the situation, humanly speaking it did not make much sense, a father of two children with a wife, I resigned from my position without even knowing how I was going to provide for my family. When we face complexities, we must keep our eyes focused on the vision that God has invested on the inside of us.

Beloved, nothing in the world can stop us from fulfilling the dreams, which God has deposited on the inside of us. *The only individual who can hinder us from carrying out our purposes in life is ourselves.* Many people blame Satan for everything that goes wrong in their lives, but they never take the time to ask God why certain things don't work out for them. Satan would be powerless if believers would begin to understand their authority in the Word of God and use that authority to get results in every area of life. The Bible says, "My people are destroyed for a lack of knowledge" (Hosea 4:6, NKJV). This means everything we desire is already in the Word of God. As we begin to study the Word of God and meditate in His Word, He will clearly reveal to us the knowledge that we lack. Therefore, we will begin to see the manifestation of His take place in our lives.

The Word of God will constantly produce results whenever believers learn to use it: with faith and power, and the Spirit who knows everything will confirm whatever we have been released on the earth. The Word of God is an instruction book for believers to live life successfully. The Word also allows us to experience life to the fullest as we walk in victory after victory. In other words, nothing is broken and nothing is lacking. I Peter 5:8 states how, the devil walks around like a roaring lion looking for whom He may devour. We need the Word of God to not only survive, but thrive.

We have to be careful not to waste most of our time concentrating on the activities of this world or living a lifestyle that is completely opposed to Christianity. I noticed that believers who spend more time entertaining themselves with technology than in the Word, wonder at the end of the day, why God never answers their prayers. Our prayers must reflect the Word of God, but we need to know the Word in order to pray the Word.

Just as we must meditate on God's Word, we must live by His Spirit. The Spirit of God is the One who identifies Christians as the children of God, so we must always try to live our lives by the Spirit of God. The Bible says,

> *"But you are not controlled by your sinful nature. You are controlled by the Spirit if you have the Spirit of God living in you. (And remember that those who do not have the Spirit of Christ living in them are not Christians at all.) Since Christ lives within you, even though your body will die because of sin, your spirit is alive because you have been made right with God."* Romans 8:9-10. (NLT)

I learned one principle in my own personal life, and it works for me all the time. Whenever I face a difficult moment in my life, I always remind myself of one thing, the sacrifice that He, Jesus, made on Calvary for my sins. If He could have gone through all that pain to save me, there is nothing Jesus Christ will not do for His children.

When we learn to rest in God's promises, there will be nothing too hard for us to endure. When we lose our focus in the word of God and fail to apply His principles, we become confused and overwhelmed. We need to remember God designed the wilderness to shape and mold His children. *People, who never face any trouble in life, would not appreciate the blessings of God.* If someone experiences hunger for several weeks, and is not able to buy food, that individual will be very sensitive toward someone who is in need. Sometime God permits situations to happen, so He can purify our hearts, and make them very sensitive toward people who are in need.

Make this decision. Every time you face challenges in life, you *choose to* always keep a positive attitude because your Father in heaven will never resign from His throne; therefore, you can rest in His promises.

CHAPTER 3
EMBRACE THE VISION

I heard a story about an elderly woman who was ninety-five years old and living in a retirement home. She became a great opera singer and people would come from all over the world just to hear her sing. One day someone asked the question, "Why didn't you use your talent at a younger age?" She explained, "When I was a young girl, I used to always dream of becoming an opera singer, but my parents told me to choose a profession that would be more supportive, because they didn't believe that I could make a living by being an opera singer. As a result, I went and took a degree in the medical field, but I hated it all my life." God has created us here on earth for a specific purpose and a divine assignment for His Kingdom. Most people live life without ever realizing the vision that God has invested within them. They never understood their identity in Christ. It is impossible to reach the destination without first being able to 'see' the path. You must first embrace the vision.

FINDING THE VISION

No one else on this planet can perform your divine assignment but you. Several years ago, before I became a born again believer in Christ, I had no idea what God's plan was for my life. One day I heard my pastor teaching about the importance of seeking the will of God for your life. As a result, I began to ask God to reveal His plan for my life. God began to unfold His purposes for my life. At first, it did not make much sense, but I continued to ask Him to reveal His plan for me. He began ordering my steps and I now see how He was preparing me to walk in all that I am doing now. Too many people spend year after year searching... looking... asking. Unfortunately, they look in all the wrong places. They don't recognize that what they are searching for God has already placed inside of them. Complacency settles in and many of us doubt the callings of God inside of us. So we search, yet never finding what we are looking for. Until we follow the path, which God desires for us, we will never find peace.

We need to find out what the plan of God is for our lives, so we can experience the favor of God. The reason why some people have not fully walked in the fullness of God's grace is that they do not understand the vision God has designed for them. God is yearning to see each of His children fulfill their callings in the Kingdom. Often in the Bible, we see great men and women of God called to accomplish a specific task. Like us, they seemed disillusioned at first. It didn't make much sense for them in the beginning. Yet, when they recognized the voice of God, they chose to believe. Belief birthed the faith to see in the spirit what was to come in the natural and they began to see what God saw. They saw themselves in the fullness of who God called them to be.

Until we begin to live our dreams and visualize what we were called to do, our dreams will never come to pass. God allows us to dream dreams because they are essential to Him. A dream is a very powerful tool God uses to show us where He is going to take us in the future. Those dreams and visions are there to direct and motivate believers, so we can fulfill our destiny on this planet. They also give us a sense of confidence that our destination has been shaped by the Almighty God. When God discloses His plan for our lives through a dream or vision, He wants us to get ourselves prepared for that task, which we must implement for His glory.

One of the most important things you can do is to ask God to unveil to you everything you will need to know about the occupation. When God calls us to perform a task, we still need to take the time to consult the Holy Spirit to make it clear to us. God may direct you to talk to someone that is already in the field. The Bible says how zeal without knowledge is not good (Romans 10:2). There are many people, who have the zeal to achieve a specific task, but they do not have the knowledge to know how to carry it out. You will never reach the next level in the life until you acknowledge that zeal and will are only half of the battle. Knowledge is key.

FAITH FOR THE VISION

When God reveals to us, through vision or dreams, that He is going to use us to accomplish something significant for His kingdom, we need to be prepared for the opposition that we will eventually face. We need to have faith that God has already given us the victory over every challenge. Moreover, Satan will try to do everything he can to take us away from the will of God. God motivates us through dreams and visions, so we can have more self-assurance in Him. When we go through a very difficult situation, sometimes God may give us a revelation from a dream. If you have walked this journey for any time, you know that sometimes we don't understand what God is doing. Nevertheless, faith is like film. It is developed in the dark. It is here that we learn to trust God for what we cannot see. Therefore, no matter what the enemy uses against us, he will not overtake us because our heavenly Father has already revealed to us in our dreams that we will have the victory.

Too often, we let negative influences steal the dream that God has deposited in us; we allow people to waste our God given gifts and talents. We allow individuals to pervert our minds with their ideologies while simultaneously diverting us from fulfilling God's plan for our lives. In addition, we allow our own failures to derail God's plan for our lives. Many people don't pursue their divine assignments because they try once and fail. They are afraid of trying a second time. We need to understand whenever we fail, God is so masterful that He can take failure and sculpt our faith. He will allow us to face situations to prepare us for bigger things. When we experienced a setback in a specific venture that we try to accomplish, instead of having a bitter attitude from that experience, ask God what is the next big prospect He has for you. God knows our future. He knows where we are going to be in the next ten years from now, so we have to keep our faith in Him and position ourselves for the blessing. When God created humanity, He gave each of us the ability to fulfill our purposes in life. We do not have to try to be somebody else or to mimic someone else just because we admire that person. Let us be an original. God gives each one of us diverse potential for the purpose of His ministry. If we understand our God given assignment, we will never again envy somebody else's gift.

Focus believer... even through failure. I have tried many things in life, where I had no success. I will never stop trying, for I know one thing. The favor of God will help me succeed in everything that I do according to His timing. I have realized that when God puts a desire in my heart, I am the only one who has the ability to perform that specific duty—nobody else can perform it like me. We need to always stay persistent in the vision that God had placed on the inside of us; sometimes, it doesn't make much sense to us, but we must always remember what God told us in the beginning.

I remember when God revealed to me to start a church. He had revealed to me where I needed to start the church. In my mind, I thought everything was going to happen very fast. I figured if God could reveal where He wanted to start the ministry, people would definitely come to join the church. What I thought was going to happen did not happen the way I expected it to happen. As a matter fact, the church did not grow for two years, and then the building where we were having services in was sold. As a result, we had to spend months without any services. I ended up losing some of the members. There were times when I got discouraged, but there was something on the inside of me, which was pushing me to keep believing in the promises of God.

When God told me to start Revelation of Church in Miami, Florida, there were people who were close to me who did not support the idea. When we dream to accomplish a task, we must prepare our minds and accept whatever affliction will come our way. As a leader, I have found myself walking alone in the plans of God. There are some occasions in my life when those closest to me did not understand the calling of God on my life. It is a very difficult situation for an individual to experience when we expect the people who are the closest to us and whom we love the most to be the first ones to help us fulfill God's destiny, but instead, they do not even recognize our callings. We must never find our certainty from people but from God only. God is the maker of all men, and He knows what He called and designed you to do.

Many people are quick to talk about what God has revealed to them in a vision. Sometimes when God reveals a vision to us, it does not mean that it is going to occur on our own time. When we share it with someone who does not even believe in God's promises, we allow that individual to feed us with negative feedback. Typically, this kind of deposit causes us to be discouraged and destroy the vision God implanted on the inside of us. God will always keep His promises, and He will bring our divine assignments into reality.

In the book of (Joshua 1:5-6), God said to Joshua, *"No one will be able to stand their ground against you as long as you live. For I will be with you as I was with Moses. I will not fail or abandon you. Be strong and courageous, for you will lead my people to possess all the land I swore to give their ancestors."* Even though, God had a responsibility to help Joshua conquer the lands, Joshua had to do his part in order for God to bring his vision to reality by staying encouraged.

"...But when God? How long God?" We often have so many questions for God. God does not always tell us *how* He is going to bring everything into existence, but we must always remember what He told us to do, and we need to stay focused on the vision He unveiled to us. We have to have a persistence mindset and a can do mentality to achieve whatever we desire in life. If we make our dreams a portion of our lives, we will be able to remain firm even when we encounter the oppositions of life. Whenever we experience setbacks, difficulties, or conflict while we are pursuing our dreams, it serves to prove just how bad we want it. How hard will you fight? People, who do not have a vision in life, will never be able to achieve anything. Don't live an unhappy life because you failed to pursue the call of God through the problems of life.

DISTORTION OF THE VISION

Distortions of divine assignments are often dressed in success. Many Christians believe just because they have been successful in a certain arena of life that they *must* be walking according to the perfect will of God. Our success in life does not automatically guarantee that God has been with us, or that we have been obedient to His will. Whenever the grace of God can flow freely in any given circumstance, we can truly identify that we are walking in His will. If we try to achieve our own tasks and don't sense the peace of God in that matter, we can be certain that God is definitely not in it. If God has called you to a specific work, He has also given you the grace to do it. He already put all the tools that you would need to perform that specific task that He has ordained you to accomplish.

Many people make the mistake modifying their assignment. Instead of utilizing the gifts and talents God has given them, so the glory of the kingdom can be manifested, they end up doing things that God did not call them to do. They assume what God had planned for their lives is not going to secure them financially. For example, if God had called them to be a high school teacher to make a difference in the lives of the youth and they say to themselves, "let me become a nurse; so I will be able to make more money." They must understand that when God was creating them, He gave them the unique ability to be a great teacher, not a nurse. I know you have met that 'nurse' who has no patience for their patients. You think to yourself... "this is NOT their calling." Precisely. God has fashioned your personality for specific tasks, which He desires for you to do. *You are who you are for a reason.*

When God created Abel and Cain, they both had different occupations. The Bible explains that Abel was a shepherd and Cain was a farmer. Since the beginning of time, God has created us with an expertise to perform the mission He designed us to execute. God never intended for anyone to live a traumatic or frustrated life. Whatever God calls us to do, He will grant us the grace and the peace to perform it. Therefore, if we are doing something in life, and we are not experiencing the grace of God in that matter, we need to ask Him if we are doing what we were called to do. I am not saying everything God called us to do is going to be easy, but what I am saying is we should not be feeling stressful or ungratified about our callings in life. *If God is the one who calls us to complete a crucial assignment, His grace will always be sufficient for us to bring it to completion.*

Don't fall victim to adult peer pressure. Many times, we try to do things that we have no business doing. We are trying to please others or at best, fit in with a particular crowd. This is when the spirit of jealousy will begin to develop in us, and if we are not careful and examine ourselves on a daily basis, Satan will use it against us. We have to keep reminding ourselves that our mission here is not for us to please people, but to do the will of God, and to carry out His assignment. We must constantly go after the purposes of God for our lives. When we try to do something God did not call us to do, we're going to have to force ourselves to remain in a position even when we are not content. There are many ministers of the Gospel, who are trying to compete with one another. Pastors are guilty of measuring their success by the success of other pastors. If a pastor buys a new building, promotes a new program or offers some new enticing ministries... the next pastor attempts to 'out do' what the previous pastor just accomplished. This competition is often at the expense of the congregation. They are pressured to push beyond their means so that their pastor can 'compete. Some pastors go as far as taking enormous loans to do what was not even ordained by God. In the end, they put themselves in debt, and then we wonder why the church is facing such a crisis.

The body of Christ needs to seek the wisdom of God more instead of competing with each other. If my brother bought a bigger building for his congregation, and I am still having church in a smaller place, I need to be thankful to God for what He had done in his life, because his success is also my success. We are ambassadors for the Kingdom. Even the devil and his demons are not fighting against each other; they stick together, and they only have one collective goal—to destroy God's people. Believers want to build up their own empire. If we call ourselves the body of Christ and there is no unity among us, we are just fooling ourselves. It is a very shameful thing to see a pastor making hateful comments about another pastor on television; Christ said that we should love one other. We must have only one collective goal—to enhance the Kingdom of God. In addition, our duty is to let the people know the greatest gift that God has given them is the gospel. In Him, there is forgiveness for their sins, because if we confess with our mouth and believe in our hearts that Christ died for our sins, we will be saved. I heard it put like this... *"Our sole business is soul business."*

We have to learn to embrace the calling of God for our lives, and we must determine to pursue His will in everything we do. God is not going to fulfill anything in our lives, which He has not authorized. When God puts a vision in us, He has the responsibility to provide for the vision on His own timing. Therefore, we need to stay focused on the task that we have to accomplish. When we experience failure, let it be an opportunity for us to learn because those who keep trying will win some day. Those who have never tried anything, they've already failed. We should never allow anyone to discourage us because of a setback we experience. Protect the vision of God in your life by walking in faith through failure. Close your ears to naysayers and open your heart to God. Declare… "Here I am, Lord. Use me." Embrace the vision and choose life with God!

CHAPTER 4
THE SELECTION OF A SPOUSE

As children of God, we must understand that before we were yet born, God had already set apart a perfect companion for each one of His children. As a pastor, people ask me the same question almost every time. *"Pastor, how can I be sure whether he/she is right for me?"* One of the most important aspects believers fail to acknowledge in dating is the sovereign plan of God and more importantly, how does this individual fit in that plan. When we engage in a relationship with someone, we have to make sure that person will fit into God's divine plan for our lives. In the previous chapter, we discussed embracing the vision of God for your life. In order to properly apply that concept, the vision of God MUST be in view when considering a mate. We must seek God and then ask some very crucial questions about this person. Let's talk more about it.

THE PRAYER

I cannot stress enough the importance of prayer in living this abundant life. It is a repeated practice you will continue to see all throughout this book. I have discovered that many people get into relationships without even consulting the Lord. Consequently, they end up hurting themselves. Prayer is quintessential in the process of selecting a mate. Let's look to sacred to the Word.

When Abraham was getting ready to look for a wife for his son Isaac, the Bible says he sent his servant on a long journey to look for a wife for his son. However, when the servant did not know how to choose a wife for his master's son, he **prayed to God** and asked him to reveal to him the right woman for Isaac (Genesis 24:12). The servant understood it would be impossible for him to recognize his master's son's wife with his natural mind. If he had not prayed to God but chosen a wife based on his wisdom, he would have made a bad decision. Because he prayed to God, God opened his eyes and showed that Rebecca was the chosen bride for Isaac.

When we pray and ask God to give us specific instructions regarding what we prayed for, we can know we are walking in the faultless will of God. We **need** God for every decision in life... every decision. We need His Spirit to guide us. It is the Spirit of God that allows us to discern the heart of an individual. God's desire to be a part of every decision is not only to guide us but also to guard us. Obedience is key to prayer. What good is it for us to pray and then disobey? What we have to do is to follow the path that He shows us... even when we do not fully understand.

What should I pray for? Great question! When we pray, and we ask of God to bring someone significant into our lives, we need to be more concerned about the spiritual characteristics. It is the most important above all other aspects of the relationship. Ask yourself... "Is there a spiritual connection between us?

God specializes in the abnormal. Often what we look for in relationships is NOT what God wants to give us. He knows what is best for us because He designed us. Consider King David. God chose him to be the King of Israel, but for several years, he was just a shepherd boy taking care of his father's sheep. He did not appear to fit the bill for a king. It seemed impossible for a shepherd boy to become king. His own father did not believe he could become the next king of Israel, but God who knew David's heart. He knew just how He designed David. God knows our abilities because He created us. Maybe God has put a special person in your life, and He wants you to marry that individual. However, when you scrutinize the individual, you think he or she is not the right person for you. Friends, understand that sometimes God is not always answering our prayer the way we intended. In God's timing, we will understand why He allowed us to go a different route instead of the route we desired. God knows our future and our personalities. Therefore, He understands what is good for His children.

One final point on prayer... We typically don't think of praying for ourselves when selecting for a mate. However, a key to our success in relationships is being personally whole and healed. We need to have a healthy love for ourselves. So many people get into relationships without even first been healed from a previous affiliation where they were hurt and wounded. It is almost unfathomable to love someone if we are carrying bitterness and resentment in our hearts. Eventually, we will end up messing up the new connection. The Bible says, "you can't put new wine in old wineskin." We have to get rid of the old wineskin first before we can use the new wineskin.

THE PICKING

The Bible says, *"God gave names to all the livestock, birds, and wild animals. But still there was no companion suitable for Adam"* (Genesis 2:20). The word "suitable" means to fit in. Too many times, we make decisions based on the outward appearance, instead of seeking the will of God and having a clear understanding about the person we passionately desire. We need to find out if the person is in the plan of God for our lives in order for that person to contribute in our future.

God unites us spiritually in order that we might experience success naturally. Before I met my wife, I used to ask God to bless me with a significant spouse because I knew I was called to be a minister of the gospel. Someone who was going to help me fulfill what God has already predestined for my life. My desire was to be with someone who was going to live her life based on the Word of God. It is very important for every believer to know that before engaging with someone, we must find out first, if the love of God has been developing inside the individual before we can actually give credence to that person. When someone operates in the love of God, that individual will produce good fruits. As a Christian, I can frankly say that the love of God is the only thing that substantiates my relationship with my wife. The love of God is the one thing that will help us to learn to forgive whenever we cannot do it on our own strength. Many believers make the mistake of marrying an unbeliever. They become convinced that they could change that person after marriage, but then later they realized that it would be impossible to change that person. When we have God's love on the inside of us, it becomes a natural thing to love one another, even though sometimes we might not agree in everything. God's love will help us overcome all natural circumstances of life. If we are in a relationship with someone, the most essential thing we need is to cry out and ask God to pour His love inside of us so we can experience God's love in the relationship.

I was talking to a young woman, and she was explaining to me that she did go out on a date for many years, since she broke up with her ex-boyfriend. She was very concerned, because she was in her late thirties. *"What do you look for in a man"*, I asked her. She gave me her "list." *"He must have a nice body with a six pack,"* she said. *"I understand a nice body, but a six-pack??? You need to lower some of your expectations just a little bit,"* I told her. When we allow God to choose the person we ought to be with, He may not give you everything you want, but He will make sure that He blesses you with someone who will love you completely. If we are only attracted to someone by the way he/she looks, we set ourselves up for failure. What will happen when the individual no longer looks the same? Looks can sometimes be deceiving, but when we allow God to shape us and mold us the way He desires us to be, we will not only look beautiful on the outside, we will be beautiful on the inside as well.

Understand this… Many people make the mistake of marrying someone because of his or her appearance. As a result, they end up divorced a few years later. When I met my wife for the very first time, I was not only concerned about the way she looked, but more importantly, her relationship with God. I believe that once we develop a healthy relationship with God, the rest will fall in place. Some people want to do it by themselves instead of allowing God to be the one to govern their steps and control their lives. God has many ways to help us meet the right mate for our future; what we need to do is to be patient, focus on His plan, and learn to know how to position ourselves for greatness.

Listen to this story. Years ago, a young woman was dating a young fellow that did not fully fulfill her fantasy, so she let him go. After many years had passed, she realized what a terrible mistake she made. That fellow was the man whom God had chosen for her, but because that young man was not educated, she aborted the plan of God. She broke up with him. Several years later, the young man went to college, graduated from theology school, and became a minister of the gospel, traveling all over world. Today, she is forty years old and very much regrets the decision she made, because no other man has asked her to marry. She missed the blessing of God.

Many people make the same mistake. We often miss the blessings of God because they are not 'packaged' he way we like. We end up rejecting God's blessing. Is it possible you are waiting on God to send someone and He already did? I heard a story about a young man, who was a Christian, and he was dating a young Christian woman. Because that young man was uneducated, one day the mother of that young woman was very disrespectful toward him and called him all kinds of names. She told the daughter not to marry the young man because she didn't think she would have a good future with him. Five years later, the young man went to college, law school, and became a lawyer. The mother of that young woman did not know what to do regarding how to ask the young man to marry her daughter. The young man didn't marry her daughter. God blessed him with an awesome young woman who wasn't concerned about materialism. We choose spouses by what we see, but God chooses for us based on what we need. I am not saying it is not important to be financially stable or even have a good physical appearance. However, we should never make these things our only priorities in life.

Many people believe when they know someone for a very long time, it automatically signifies this is the will of God for them to be together. When God calls two people to be together, it does not mean they have to date for a very long time. What is essential is to know the will of God in the relationship before making any decisions. God knows the beginning and the end, so if He calls us to be with someone, He knows what He is doing. Just obey. God is not limited by how long you've known someone. When God puts two people together, His vision must be their priority. In a marriage, if only one spouse is willing to live life according to God's will, there will always be conflict between them. Let's say one partner trusts God for everything he/she is doing, but the other spouse only makes decisions according to his/her natural instincts. It will create a dilemma between the two of them.

True story... Years ago, I was dating a young woman. She was a believer, but when we were dating, we used to argue about everything. No matter what we talked about, there was always a disagreement between us. Finally, we broke up and went our separate ways. I was hurt and many questions came to mind. I did not understand why it happened. Beloved, just because you're dating another Christian brother or sister, it doesn't automatically mean it's the Lord's doing. *God will give us a mate, who will help us fulfill His purposes for our lives.* If a person does not contribute to the plan of God for your life, you need to seek God whether this is the one for you.

While I don't believe lengthy courtships guarantee success, I do believe you need to spend as much time as possible with each other before you can get serious about getting married. When I say "spending time," I am not talking about how long you have known the individual. It is not about the quantity of time more than the quality of time you spend with someone.

THE PROVISION

According to statistics, the number one cause of divorce in the United States is financial instability. Money is perhaps the biggest challenge families' face today. Many wives and husbands have walked away from their homes because of the circumstances of life. As a result, the institution of marriage has lost its value. People are depressed because they cannot pay their bills. Some Christians are even compromising their faith because of the economic demands they have to endure. The wife complains because her husband loses his job. The husband is frustrated because he does not know what to do. Consequently, there is no happiness in the home, so the marriage falls apart.

You have to trust God to provide financially in your marriage. One day I did not have any money, but I was praying to God to help me. While I was driving, a car came from out of nowhere and hit the rear of my car. I got out making sure that everything was all right. Thank God, the vehicle wasn't damaged. The driver told me that she was very sorry and she gave me one hundred dollars! We didn't have a penny in our pocket. God came through for us and blessed us with one hundred dollars. When our marriages are built on the solid rock, no matter what we encounter in life, it will not be shaken. The Bible says, *"Though the rain comes in torrents and the flood waters rise and the rain beats against that house, it won't collapse because it is built on a rock"* (Matthew 8:25). In any relationship, Jesus needs to be the solid rock. When we make Jesus the center of our marriage, whenever we face challenges in life, He will always rescue us because we allow Him to be the foundation of our marriage.

The Bible says," *Trust in the Lord with all your heart; do not depend on your own understanding. Seek His will in all you do, and He will direct your path.*" (Proverbs 3:5-6) God wants us to depend on Him for everything. The truth is we often substitute security in God for stability in others. It's why our demands are so high. They must have a college degree, a great bank account, or a very prestigious occupation. Then and only then can we consider endorsing that individual as consideration to be a husband or a wife. We judge people by what we can see with our natural eyes. If we really think about it, there is no such thing as being financially secure. We can go to sleep rich and wake the next day broke. However, when we find our security in the Lord Jesus, there is nothing to worry about. He knows our beginning and our future. Therefore, He will always protect us and provide for us even in time of recession.

THE PERSPECTIVE

Beloved, there will be times in your marriage relationship when it may seem that it will not last when we see things from our perspective. We must strive to have the mind of Christ to see things from God's perspective. Know that when we see or marriage from God's perspective, we will see how He is making it better. This is the reason I encourage you to always put God first in your relationships, whether it is social, marital or casual. God needs to be involved in everything we do, so He can show us how to use the wisdom He puts in us. God's direction is not without opposition. It is for us to trust Him and not abort His instructions.

Dear brothers and sisters, if we want to have a successful relationship, we need to make Jesus the source of our lives. It is necessary for us to observe these things before we get into a bond with someone; we need to take notice if that person is concerned more about spirituality than the things of this world. If both of us are not in line with God's Word, the relationships will become very stressful. In addition, if God is not the one who rules the marriage, there will always be confusion.

As we put God first and learn to appreciate all the beautiful gifts He has given us, the anointing will always stream into our affiliation with one another. We should never put our trust in things or men, neither in what we possess. All these things will someday fade away.   When God chooses to bless us with someone who loves Him, and loves the things of God, that individual will certainly love his/her spouse.

It is important for both spouses to see things from God's perspective, so they can experience the grace of God in everything we do. Jesus said, "*A house divided against itself will not stand.*" (Matthew 12:25) When two people in a relationship acknowledge God in everything, there will never be any obstacle too immense for them to conquer. Satan will try to put a spirit of division in every believer's home. When we pray together as a couple, we allow God to reveal Himself to us. Collectively, we will understand the heart of God, and what He desires for the marriage. If one person in the relationship has a prayer life, and the other one does not have a prayerful lifestyle, Satan will have access to the spouse that is not spending time communicating with God. It is often through that person that Satan brings marital opposition.

When husband and wife trust God to direct their lives in everything they do and devote themselves in prayer with a joyful heart, and a thankful mindset, God will reveal to them His secret plan for the marriage. In addition, the favor of God will rest upon them eternally. It is not possible to have a successful marriage if God is not the center of that marriage. God is the maker of every man and every woman. He knows our thoughts, but if we do not develop a relationship with Him, how can He disclose to us when something is not going well in our marriage? Sometimes we may think that we have the answers for everything that is happening in our relationships. If God is not the one who reveals to us certain things, we will spend our time and money looking for the source of the problem but will never find it. It takes the Holy Spirit to make it clear to us. My friends, we need to devote ourselves to the things of God. As we make Him the source in our marriage or our interaction, we will win all the times.

Many people got married, but they didn't make the Word of God the establishment and final authority of the marriage. As a result, when they face unexpected conditions, instead of trusting the Word of God, they begin to blame each other for the hardships they have encountered. If we allow God to direct our path in our relations, He will straighten the rough places in our lives. If we make Him the center of our marriage by allowing Him to be the pilot of our everyday life, we shall overcome any hardship that we do not comprehend. God understands our heart's desires; however, we need to ask ourselves if those desires are going to benefit our marriage, or will, they become a burden for the marriage? God will never fulfill any promise, which He has not promised to us. Many believers expect God to carry out their fleshly desires even though He has nothing to do with them, and if He does not answer their prayer, they get discouraged and upset with God. When we seek after the will of God in every aspect of our lives, and yet afflictions occur in our relationships, God has the responsibility to reveal it to us what is not working properly in our marriage.

The Power of God's Perspective: In 2005, I had an encounter with God in a vision. He showed me how He was going to use me in the ministry. God said to me, "These things that I showed you will not happen instantly, but you will have to suffer many trials before they come to pass. I want you to read your Bible and do not go to work." At that time, I had just gotten married. My wife at the time was pregnant with our son, and she was the only one working. It was difficult to understand how God was preparing me to be a minister of the gospel.

We went through the worst moments in our marriage. I remember there were times, I would go look for jobs, but I could not find one. Sometimes my wife would wake up in the middle of the night and start crying because she could not understand the situation. I did not know what to do. I was very frustrated and very angry with God for allowing me to go through that terrible condition. I could not pay my rent, so I felt so helpless. There were moments when I wished that I were dead. Family members talked about me, as if I were the most wanted on national television. I faced enormous criticism from family members because it did not make sense to them. I remember one day, as I arrived home from a job interview, my mother- in-law's friend called my house and disrespected me. *"You don't care about your family. How can a husband let his pregnant wife take care of him? You are a loser,"* she said. At that moment, I lost my cool and many things went through my head. I wanted to avenge that woman, but the Holy Spirit began to remind me of the works that He was doing through me, and why He allowed these things to happen to me.

I was going through the molding process. He was shaping my character to be a spiritual leader for His Kingdom. That conversation transpired on a Tuesday. On Sunday while I was in church and the pastor was talking about how we must learn to forgive our enemies. He gave these illustrations about Jesus Christ and how He forgave even the people who had mistreated Him. The Holy Spirit began to convict me about what I was thinking of doing to this woman, so I made a decision that was not easy for me. I got on my knees, and I asked God to help me to forgive her.

Our marriage had become very dire; as a result, I cried out to God and asked Him to help me in this predicament. It was a very painful experience for me because I knew that I had heard the voice of God, but nobody believed me. My best friend and I began to pray almost every day seeking after the will of God, so I could get a breakthrough in my financial difficulty. Instead of finding a job, so I could provide for my family, God told me to start a Bible study in my living room, so I did as I was told. As a result, my ministry was birthed through pain and suffering. I began to have a yearning to see people delivered from the hands of the enemy, and to encourage married couples to always acknowledge God in their relationships.

When God revealed to me to open Revelation of Church, those closest to me could not fully see the vision. I remember starting the church without much support. It was a very hard situation for me to deal with. We must understand that we have an adversary, and his plan is to bring confusion into our marriage, families, and lives, so he can take us away from the will of God. Satan would be powerless if we believers were determined to engage ourselves in the Word of God. It is in His Word that we begin to understand His will. We must always stay on guard and have a warrior mentality, so we can fight against the schemes of the enemy. We must fight for our marriage. God said, "It is not good for man to be alone." Therefore, He created marriage for our benefit. We should never allow the enemy to get us discouraged and give up in our relationships.

Sometimes, God does not explain to us the reason why we go through everything we face. Many times God will test our faith to see how much we really trust in Him. We have to remember our Father has control over everything, in heaven, on earth and under the earth. When we made a vow before God that we're going to spend the rest of our lives together, we need to remind ourselves of that vow, which has been recorded in the book of heavens. We said we would live our lives for better and for worst; this covenant should not be broken unless death takes place. People of God, we need to educate ourselves before we give ourselves into marriage. When we decide to live our lives exclusively to the will of God, we must remember Satan is not going to be pleased with us. I believe the reason many Christians divorce is because they go to church every

Sunday, but they never make a decision to apply the Word in their lives. If we only hear the Word of God, and never make a decision to apply it in our lives, we are just like sick individuals who went to the doctor but refused to take the medication the doctor prescribed for the sickness.

The only time a marriage is going to be successful is when two individuals commit to live their lives based on the Word of God. Let God's Word guide you to marriage and guard you in your marriage.

CHAPTER 5
LET'S TALK ABOUT SEX!

I want to take the time to elaborate about one of the most sensitive subjects that the church has failed to discuss.   Sex is very significant in the marriage relationship.   It is very important for husbands and wives to have a healthy sexual relationship. If it were not so, God would not have required us to be married in order for us to be sexually intimate. God created marriage to be a beautiful thing, and *He created sex*, so we can enjoy each other's company. Until we understand how intimacy with one another plays a big role in marriage, we will never experience the blessings of God to the fullness.   Lasting marriages honor the significance of having a good sexual relationship.

When we say "yes" to marriage, we enter into a sacred covenant where we literally give ourselves completely to each other: bodies, life, possessions and so forth. Our desire should be to please each other and live for each other. It's all a part of this holy covenant.

THE PURPOSE OF SEXUAL INTIMACY

What is so important about sex? Think about life before marriage. When we were single, we could not wait to get married. We used to think about the good times we would experience. We spent enormous times preparing for the day of the wedding. Some spent their entire life saving themselves for that beautiful day. At that occasion, we were in love; we were willing to do anything to please the other person, and we used to talk about everything and anything. Whenever we saw each other, we were very joyful and had butterflies in our stomachs. As time transpired, what we once adored, we now just live with... What was so valuable to us, we now disvalue. We should always keep reminding ourselves of the reasons we took the vows and always remember how we used to love spending quality time together, have insignificant conversations, cuddle and laugh, as nothing was more important than to be with one another.

God created sex in the marriage because He had a purpose in mind. The truth is, it is not good for a believer to deprive her husband or his wife of sexual intercourse. God created sex to be pleasurable, procreative and spiritual. When we take away that special fulfillment found only in sexual intimacy, we are disobeying God's divine creative order. We are choosing to disregard all of His instruction according to His Word as it pertains sex. It pleases God to see His children obeying Him and govern their lives by His instructions. When we decide to love our spouses and build our marriages based on the Word of God, we position our homes to be guided and guarded.

When we neglect sexual intimacy, we allow Satan to have access to tempt us. He will use that void against us, so he can bring conflicts into the marriage. When one of the individuals is not satisfied sexually, it will bring about frustration in the marriage. Not only will it bring frustration but feelings of rejection. Rejection often leads to infidelity. The Bible clearly mentions the wife's body as belonging to her husband; likewise, the husband's body belongs to the wife, and they will become one flesh. Therefore, we should never deprive each other from sexual intimacy. God understands the significance of sexual intimacy in the marriage. It is a vital thing. We must make it a priority.

The problem many people have in their marriages is that they do not distinguish what to prioritize. When we know our priorities, we will begin to invest more time in what is important instead of wasting our time in the insignificant things of life. We must recognize what to value the most in order for our marriages to be successful. In marriages, some wives prioritize their children more than they do their husbands. Some people prefer to put their job or social activities before their marriages such as spending countless hours online chatting with friends. All of these activities are to bring some sense of satisfaction. God designed sexual intimacy to be satisfying fulfilling part of our married lives. Many couples in the church have complained that their spouses who do not take the time to be intimate with them. It is the reason why the rate of divorce in the church is the same as the world.

CHALLENGES TO SEXUAL INTIMACY

Why do we allow the circumstances of life make us forget the value of being married? When we allow Satan to govern our minds with the temporary things of this world, we hinder the power of God to manifest in our marriage. God's plan for believers is to see us making progress in every aspect of life, so the Kingdom of God will continue to make progress. When we allow the enemy to make us lose focus in the most essential things of our lives, we go down our own paths. We will chose paths contrary to this truth… *we understand that our marriages are most valuable to God.* Apart from renewing our minds in God's Word, we will downplay the necessity of maintaining sexual intimacy with our spouses, and the significant role it plays in our marriage. We should do whatever it took to keep excitement and sexual intimacy in our relationships.

When we face adversities in life, let it be an opportunity for us to grow instead of withdrawing from each other. If God is the source of our marriage, we need to let Him be the one who supplies for our needs instead of blaming one another for what happens in our lives. I met a man years ago. He explained to me the difficulties that he was facing in his marriage, and how his wife lost the passion of having sexual interaction. The man was a pastor of a small church in California. They were going through financial difficulties that caused his wife to become very frustrated. She was no longer interested in the marriage. She began to withdraw herself from her husband, and reject him every time he wanted to make love with her. He mentioned how hard it was for him to endure the temptations, which he faced from the women in his congregation. However, that was not important to his wife at that moment; she was only concerned about the bills, not her marriage. If this pastor's wife had understood that her happiness was not based on how she felt about her situation and that God was the one in control, she would have had the peace of God to overcome her circumstances.

God's Word is not just for Sunday morning. If we are to be true followers of Christ, true Christians, we must not only hear the Word but be doers. Our faith must have shoes that we walk in... Oh how different story above would have been if only she did more than read about trusting God. When we face hardships in our marriage, instead of blaming everyone else (especially our spouses) for our problems, we need to seek the counsel of God through His Spirit to show us what He wants us to learn. It is possible that God is giving you an opportunity to build up your faith, or perhaps He is doing something new in your life. It's not that we don't but instead of trusting God to disclose the reason why they were going through that financial difficulty, she blamed her husband for everything that was wrong in her life. She had allowed Satan to enter into the marital covenant, and because of that, she gave an opportunity for adultery to take place in the marriage. People sometimes know what to do, but they choose to disobey the directives of God's Word. They would rather walk in rebellion against God and disobey the voice of the Holy Spirit. One of the greatest sins a believer can ever commit is to know what to do but choose not to do it. (James 4:17)

Another prohibition in sexual intimacy is satisfaction with your covenant partner. Women can be very troubled when their husbands cannot satisfy their sexual needs. As men of God, we need to be mindful of these things, so we do not become so spiritually minded and forget the natural things that God would like us to fulfill in our marriage. I was talking to a young woman who had been married for more than seven years. She told me that she had been very unhappy in her marriage because her husband didn't fulfill her sexual desires and that she had never reached orgasm when having sex with her husband.

"Pastor I am only 32 years old. I need to enjoy myself. I have not had any sexual contact with him for more than three months because of this situation," she said.

After some further research, I discovered that there were many women who are not interested in making love with their husbands. I interviewed several Christian women about intimacy in their marriage. "Why don't you enjoy sex with your husbands?" I asked them.

"Whenever I am having sex with my husband, I have never experienced an orgasm. He only wants to satisfy himself," said the women whom I interviewed. Church we have a problem! We must learn how to compromise if we really want to have a successful marriage. When we do not take the time to fulfill each other's needs, we fail to fulfill the scriptures.

God created sex in the marriage to be pleasurable and spiritual. When we take away that special fulfillment called sex in the marriage, we are telling God that we know better than He does. Thus, we make a decision not to obey Him regarding what He says about marriage. It pleases God so much to see His children are willing to obey Him and govern their lives by His instructions. When we decide to love our spouses and build our marriages based on the of God, He will make sure no weapon formed against our marriages will prosper. The problem many people have in their marriages is that they do not distinguish what to prioritize. When we know our priorities, we will begin to invest more time in what is important instead of wasting our time in the insignificant things of life. We must recognize what to value the most in order for our marriages to be successful. In marriages, some wives prioritize their children more than they do their husbands. Some people prefer to put their job or social activities before their marriages such as spending countless hours online chatting with friends.

I have heard story after story how married couples are irritated that their spouses are no longer spending enough time with them because they are spending most of their time on their computers. If we are not careful, Satan will utilize those things to distract us and probably destroy our marriages. When we decide not to pay attention concerning what God says about marriage, we grant Satan access to control our lives.

POINTERS FOR SEXUAL INTIMACY

If you are a married man, and you are reading this book, I am going to give you some tips that will help you save your marriage. Listen brothers, women do not react the same way as we do. First, when it comes to sexual activities, we need to make plans in advance when we are going to make love to our wives. Preplanning helps to make it an enjoyable experience. Secondly, we need to create a lovely atmosphere. If she is working that day, call her during the day to let her know how much you miss her and how beautiful she is. Tell her she is a blessing from God to you. Thirdly, ask her if there is any housework she would like you to do before she comes home. If there were some dirty dishes in the sink, wash those dishes before she gets home. If you are a man that knows how to cook, cook her preferred meal. When she gets home, massage her feet. I do understand that sometimes we may not have the time to do all these things, but we need to take the time to please our wives.

I am willing to provide these tips because I believe they will help your wife to be in the mood to make love to you. As husbands and spiritual leaders in the home, we must learn how to satisfy our wives sexually and take the time to acknowledge her needs in the relationship. Husbands, we need to learn how to take time to caress our wives very slowly and gently with passion, while talking romantically in her ear. Be willing to do whatever it takes your wife to experience ecstasy. Take some time for foreplay before having sexual intercourse. If you take the time to communicate with her, she will respond accordingly, and it will be much easier for her to experience orgasm. As a result, you do not have to be the one pressuring her for sex whenever you desire it.

The problem with most men is that we have a selfish mindset, which is why we do not take the time to please our wives. Some women have also complained that their husbands don't last long in bed. Let me also give you some tips to last longer in bed. Whenever you make love to your wife, focus on meeting her needs first. Learn to control your thoughts by not thinking too much about her body. As a result, you will last longer. If you focus too much on her body at that specific moment, you will experience satisfaction before she does. Sex is necessary for both parties to enjoy together. We are honoring our heavenly Father when we walk in love in our relationship, and when we take time to meet each other's needs.

You might ask yourself why talk about sex so much? To answer your question, it's because there are many men in the body of Christ, who do not know how to take the time to make love to their wives, and to gratify their sexual needs. Husbands whenever you make love to your wives, the best thing you can do is to ask her questions: ask her what does she like the most when you make love to her, and ask her how she wants you to caress her, where to touch her more, or to embrace her more. Every woman has a very sensitive part in her body that she prefers her husband caress the most. Husbands, we need to be aware of our wife's sensitive spot. Therefore, we will be able to spend more time touching her in that area, so she can also enjoy having sex. I understand there are some women, who take more time to experience orgasm than others do, but if you are familiar with her sensitive spot and spend most of the time caressing her there, you can make her content very easily.

Whenever I have someone come to me and tell me, "Pastor, I haven't had any sexual intercourse with my wife or husband for more than two months," it's a big issue, and needs to be fixed. In this situation, depression could lessen the desire for a sexual intimacy in the relationship. What I usually suggest to people is to pray to God, so He can expose the source of the problem. Satan's plan is to bring division into the relationship, so one of the spouses can go the opposite way against the will of God for that marriage. Think about a man who is not happy at home, because his wife is always too tired to have sex with him. If this man is working in an environment where there are many single women he will most likely fall into temptation. What Satan is doing is having power over the wife's mind, and using that against her husband to demolish the home. I gave this illustration, because I want the body of Christ to know how important this issue is.

We need to learn how to fight the enemy and to use Godly wisdom in our marriage... even in sex. This is why we need to inform ourselves about marriage and know how to identify the deception of the devil. We can only do these things by spending time in God's Word. As mentioned earlier, we can not only read it, but apply it. Jesus indicted the religious leaders of His day for being well read in the law but applied very little. (Luke 12:1) Jesus said, "Beware of the yeast of the Pharisees—beware of their hypocrisy." The Word of God was written for believers to put into application whether it is in good time or bad time.

CHAPTER 6

ESCAPE FROM TEMPTATION

"Lead us not in to temptation but deliver us from evil." (Matthew 6:13a) Typically when we hear the word, temptation, we think of some type of sexual connotation or deviation. Temptation can occur in numerous forms of life; we can be enticed by power, money, or sex. The question is what we will do when we get tempted. The most important thing for us to do is to be geared up and understand what we must do in order for us to stay away from the temptations of this world.

POWER IN THE WORD

Without a doubt, a consistent echo throughout this entire book is our absolute dependency and obedience to God's Word. Without it, we would be lost. We could not begin to please God and contend with the devil without the Word of God. We have to stay committed to study the Word of God. Studying the scriptures is number one for believers to be prepared in handling enticements. When we meditate on the Word of God, our thoughts and minds begin to transform and conform to the way in which God desires for us to think. Once the Word of God is rooted on the inside of us, we will be ready to face anything the enemy throws at us.

It was with the Word of God that the Son of God, Jesus Christ, defeated Satan and conquered temptation. Satan tempted Jesus immediately following his fasting for 40 days and 40 nights in the wilderness. Follow me to Luke 4:3-4…

> *The devil said to Him, "If you are the Son of God change this stone into a loaf of bread." But Jesus told Him, "No! The scriptures say People need more than bread for their life."*

Jesus understood Satan's focus was to use that specific occasion to try to take Him out of the will of God. However, when we face these situations in our own lives, we need to know how to escape from them, and to be able to handle them from a biblical standpoint. When Satan tried to entice our Lord and Savior Jesus Christ in the wilderness, Jesus had to handle Satan with the scriptures. He was weak, hungry, and tired, but He did not allow His condition to control Him. Jesus (The Word Incarnate) was submitted to the Word even in dire hunger.

When we nurture our soul with the Word of God, it becomes very easy for our flesh to become submissive to the things of God. It is necessary for believers to preoccupy their thinking with the things of God, which give life to the soul. If we make ourselves available for the purposes of God, and we endeavor to fulfill His plan in our lives, we will not have the desire to be concerned about feeding our flesh. The Word of God is a weapon believers need to use in every arena of life. If we know how to use the scripture the right way, we will destroy those bondages in our lives. "Life and death is in the power of our tongue."

The Word of God has the power to destroy the wicked things of this world, which Satan brings against God's people. Sometimes, in order for us to overcome temptation, we must accept being strange in some areas. As believers, we need to take a stand and do what is right even when it's difficult. People in the world will do whatever it takes in order for them to have success, however, we must be determined to suffer for God. When we have all the reasons to do that which is wrong, we must decide to do the right thing. God will always honor us. The Bible says, "*If you love God, you will obey Him.*" It means that when we walk away from temptations, we really prove to God that we truly love Him, and we want to follow His way instead of our own ways.

One of the books I would recommend for you to read every time you get up in the morning is the book of Proverbs in the Old Testament. This book can help you develop wisdom and understanding as you walk with God. When I was struggling with sexual sin as a new believer, I used to study the book of Proverbs almost every day, so I could learn how to handle the enticements, which Satan used against me. So the more I read my Bible, the stronger I became in my Christian walk. Since then I've been free from that bondage. Most people are waiting for God to do something for them, but God is sitting on His throne waiting for us to pick up our Word and overcome whatever situation needs to be conquered. When we get tempted in a specific area, it will be very hard for us to walk away from it initially. However, if you decide to obey God by resisting the temptation, it will be easier for us to stand firm and obey the Word the next time you get tempted.

God wants His children to have a courageous mentality. He will help us to conquer any addiction. However, we must be boldly faithful to His way. God chose a man named Joshua, who was Moses' assistant to lead the people of Israel to the promise land. Before Moses died, he charged Joshua to be the next man in line to lead the Israelites. One day the Lord spoke to Joshua and told him to lead his people to the Jordan River into the land that He'd given them.

> *"I promise you what I promised to Moses; no one will be able to stand their ground against you as long as you live. For I will be with you as I was with Moses. I will not fail or abandon you. Be strong and courageous, for you will lead my people to possess all the land I swore to give their entire ancestor. Be strong and very courageous. Obey all the laws Moses gave you. Do not turn away from them. And you will be*

successful in everything you do." (Joshua 1:1-9).

In these scriptures, God asked Joshua to be strong and very courageous twice. It explains that even when God is going to fulfill His promises in our lives, we must do our part by standing firm on His Word.

ENGAGE IN PRAYER

When we need to develop a prayerful lifestyle by communicating with God on a daily basis, our intimacy with God will begin to intensify by being in His presence. It will help us to remain in the spiritual realm at all times. Therefore, we won't allow the things of this world to distract us from the plan of God for our lives. When we constantly remain in prayer, we are crucifying our flesh without even taking any notice of it, and our spirit man will become stronger and be ready to do the will of God. Nevertheless, when we fail to spend time in prayer, it becomes very difficult for our flesh to obey God, and to overcome temptation. Our natural man takes over our spiritual man. As a result, we end up doing things that we have no business doing are being controlled by our natural man. Whenever, we decide not to spend time in prayer or reading our Bible, we even lose control of our tongues and say things that we will later regret. We should never allow ourselves to be controlled by our emotions. When Jesus Christ was here on the earth, He prayed and fasted He could commune with His Father, while simultaneously reflecting His Father's character on earth by the way He lived His life. When we pray, we need to take time to listen to the voice of God, so He can reveal to us the area that we need to better ourselves.

The mistake most people make when they are praying is that they do all the talking; however, they never take the time to listen to what God has to say about their issues. Sometimes, God wants to answer our prayer right after we finish talking to Him, but because we fail to take a moment to listen to what He has to say, we miss out on the answer.

When we pray, we need to ask God constantly to kill our fleshly desires.   If we can kill our fleshly desires, we will be able to control the destructive emotions.

EXPECT POINTS OF WEAKNESS

Some of us need to ask God for His spiritual wisdom and spiritual discernment, so we do not become too naïve in our faith. One of the main reasons why people face temptation is because they do not know how to control their environments. Controlling our environments means to choose the people with whom we need to socialize. There is an adage that says, "Show me your friend and I will tell you your future." It is very fundamental for us to know the people with whom we associate ourselves, because people can play a big role in our lives. Let's say you are a Christian married-man.   All of your friends are unbelievers. When you are talking with those friends, all they talk about is how many different women they have been with. Eventually, they will influence you with the same way of thinking. Never allow people to dump their trash into your mind.

Consider practical wisdom in expecting point of weakness. If you are a married person who works with a very attractive person, you have no business trying to develop any close relationship with that person. I know married women who've decided to go to lunch with male coworkers almost every day, and one day they wake up asking themselves how they ended up in adultery with those individuals. I am not saying when we are married that we should not socialize with other people. What I am saying is do not open up and begin to share our personal lives with someone we are not supposed to.

We need to understand that habits can have a big impact in our lives. When we spend time-sharing our personal lives with someone other than our spouses, there is a possibility that we can begin to develop a sentiment for that person. It is very important for husband and wife to learn to communicate as friends and be able to talk about anything, so they can prevent the risk of sexual temptation in the workplace. The majority of infidelity cases start in the workplaces. Sometime people spend so much time at work that they do not have time for their own family. They work too many hours and spend too much time working with an individual, so they begin to develop a lustful desire toward that individual.

We have to be wise enough, so we do not let our emotions make us do things that are not in the will of God for our lives. While you are reading this book if you know there is something you are doing which might destroy your marriage, you need to turn to the right direction and do the right thing, because nothing is more valuable for God than to see you having a successful marriage. If there is something that you do not like about your spouse, do not go to work and discuss it with a single woman, and if you are a married woman do not share your problems with a male friend. When we are in the marriage covenant with someone, everyone else that we are associating with should have his or her limit. It is very important for us to know whom we should talk with, and who to trust to share our personal life. There are married men, who take advantage of married sisters, because they know that they are going through a difficult moment in their marriage. Instead of supporting them spiritually, they take advantage of them and play with their emotions. Let me make this clear. It is wrong to take sexual advantage of an emotionally unstable woman who is going through marital difficulties.

Years ago, before I got married, I was living in Orlando, Florida in a very small apartment. There was a woman I used to talk with. She was older than I was. One day she came to my apartment and told me that she was very lonely because her husband traveled a lot because of his job. I was tempted to sleep with her, but the Holy Spirit convinced me that I was thinking of doing evil by taking advantage of her current condition. ***Sometimes we fall into sins because we are not honest*** *with ourselves*. If you are in a situation where you are battling with a certain addiction, the first thing you need to do is to be sincere, pray and ask God to show you away of escape.

Here's another true story. There was a married woman, who was going through a difficult time in her marriage. She worked with a very attractive male coworker. She told me that the male coworker was very nice. As result, she developed deep feelings toward the man. The woman was a believer filled with the Spirit of God. She told me that she did not intend to fall into sin. However, she was going through a very hard time in her marriage. Every time she would go to her husband, he would push her away. He was never in the mood to make love to her. This is why she began to develop lustful desires toward the man at work, but she was honest with herself and understood that it was not acceptable for her to develop lustful desires for another man. She went into a period of prayer and fasting, crying out to God to help her deal with the situation. God answered her prayer by giving her a way of escape. The man was transferred to another location. What I learned from her story is that she was very sincere with God by asking Him to help her escape temptation. The Bible tells us that God will always create a way to escape whenever we get tempted. Nevertheless, we must be eager to seek God's face earnestly in our prayers, so He can deliver us when we face temptations.

Anticipate temptations to be based on your weaknesses. One thing we need to do is to stay away from any foolish conversation that is not aligned with the Word of God. I understand it will never be possible to control what people talk about; however, we can take control of what we listen to. Some people are addicted to online pornography because they cannot resist the temptation of being away from the computer. If you have that kind of weakness, you must restrain yourself from having access to the internet on your computer until you have the ability to conquer that addiction. Create accountability by placing the computer in a room where everyone in your household can view it. In the meantime, ask God to give you the strength to overcome that addiction.

A recent convert in my early twenties, I was addicted to pornography. I prayed and asked God to deliver me from that addiction. One day while I was watching the Trinity Broadcasting Network (TBN), God talked to me through a minister of the Gospel about getting rid of anything that caused me to sin. Consequently, I had a video in my room, which I used to watch. Convicted by the Holy Spirit, I had to destroy that video tape.

I share this testimony because in order for us to be free from any addiction, we must be determined to be free. Nobody will experience freedom by wishing to have freedom. It is a decision that needs to begin on the inside. We must learn to fight against the evil spirit that is attacking us declaring our victory while we are praying to be set free. Whenever temptation comes our way, we must do the best we can to conquer the plan of the enemy because we have the power of God living within us. We choose life!

The Word of God is a weapon, which believers need to use in every arena of life. If we know how to use the scripture the right way, we will destroy those bondages in our lives. "Life and death is in the power of our tongue." The Word of God has the power to destroy the wicked things of this world, which Satan brings against God's people. Sometimes, in order for us to overcome temptation, we must accept being strange in some areas. Let's say, you are working for a company, and you are a single Christian mother. Your boss Tom, who is married, calls you into his office and starts to flirt with you. He asks you to go on a date with him. In addition, he mentions to you there is a new position open in the company, and if you decide to go out with him, you will be the first one in line to be hired for the job. You would be making much more money than what you are currently making, as a single mother the promotion would be helpful. As believers, we need to take a stand and do what is right even when it's difficult. People in the world will do whatever it takes in order for them to have success; however, we must be determined to suffer for God. When we have all the reasons to do that which is wrong, but we decide to do the right thing, God will always honor us. The Bible says, "If you love God, you will obey Him." It means that when we walk away from temptations, we really prove to God that we truly love Him, and we want to follow His way instead of our own ways.

CHAPTER 7
FORGIVENESS

Forgiveness has become a very difficult thing for people to address. Unforgiveness has become one of the most common sins with which Christians in the church struggle. Jesus clearly said, "If you don't forgive your brother and sister, I will not forgive you also." Forgiving someone is not something we decide to obey or not, it is a mandatory command with which we must comply. The question is why do we need to forgive?

WHY FORGIVE?

We do not forgive, because we feel like it or not, but because it is a command from God that every believer needs to implement in his or her life. When Jesus was on the earth, He had many unfair things happened to Him, but He learned to forgive because He was walking in the love of God. Jesus was determined to display the character of His Father. *The primary reason God wants His children to learn to forgive is that He desires for us to be identified as the children of God*. Whatever Jesus had demonstrated when He was here on earth was a display of what was accomplished in heaven. Therefore, His aspiration was to do the will of God 'on earth as it was in heaven.' Jesus walked in love, because His Father was love. He performed miraculous signs because His Father was a miracle maker. Everything He did was in the will of God.

Forgiveness plays a big role in a believer's life. While Jesus was on the cross, He prayed and asked God to forgive those who had crucified Him. On the other hand, when it comes to Christians, we struggle with forgiving those who have wronged us. We become upset, bitter and angry. I am not saying forgiving someone is something which is easy to do, but I would suggest that we should at least pray and ask God to help us to have a forgiving Spirit.

There was tragedy that happened to a Christian sister that I worked with at World Changers International church in Atlanta, Georgia. Her daughter was stabbed and killed by her boyfriend. I remember how strong she was even after losing her own daughter. She was a prayer warrior, and a very courageous woman of God. I remember asking her, how did she have the strength to forgive this man. *"God is real. I have experienced the love of God in my life for the very first time, and He gave me the strength to forgive,"* she said. If this woman could experience a tragic situation like this one and God give her the strength to forgive that person, what about us? The Holy Spirit can only exercise this kind of forgiveness supernaturally. The Holy Spirit came upon her and gave her the ability to carry out this kind of forgiveness. The Holy Spirit is the one who helped her overcome these painful occurrences. It would be impossible for anyone to forgive an individual in the stage of killing your own daughter. No one would ever be able to forgive someone to that extent. One key insight I have learned from her tragedy is that she didn't want to carry any bitterness in her heart. "I want to be free," she said. Forgiving this person was actually for her own benefit. When we release pains and hurts in the hand of God, we release ourselves from being in a self-imposed prison. If she had kept this man in her heart for years, she would end up living a miserable life and carry out resentment toward the person who had killed her daughter.

Many people who have been abused sexually as a child have held pains and resentments for many years. As result, it becomes very difficult for them to trust anyone because they have not forgiven the individuals who abused them. They tend to carry those memories in their relationships. When a woman has been sexually abused as a child, there is a possibility that she can become very traumatized by that experience and could affect her sexual relationship with her husband. Sometimes, it could be very painful to let go of someone who has hurt us. However, we need to know that we do not forgive because that person deserves our forgiveness, but because we love Jesus and want to follow His footsteps in everything we do. God knew that it would not be easy for us to forgive. However, He made available to us a helper who can help us overcome these things.

The Holy Spirit is our helper and our comforter. If we try to forgive with our own strength, we will always fail, but with the help of the Holy Spirit, we can do all things. The Holy Spirit is the power of God living on the inside of every believer; in other words, God's expects us to love in a supernatural way. When we have God's kind of love on the inside of us, we will be able to love people even when they do not deserve it. **God's love is unconditional.** This is the kind of love that we received the moment we were born again. When we received Jesus Christ as our Lord and Savior, the Holy Spirit birthed something new on the inside of us, giving us new life from heaven, which can only come from God. *"Most assuredly, I say to you, unless one is born of water and the Spirit, he cannot enter the kingdom of God.* [6] *That which is born of the flesh is flesh, and that which is born of the Spirit is spirit" Jesus said.* (John 3: 5-6) If we do not have the Holy Spirit living within us, it will be impossible for us to produce any spiritual fruit. Therefore, we need to pray and ask God to give us a heart that is sensitive toward the things of God. As a result, we will begin to produce the fruit of the Spirit such as love, kindness, forgiveness, gentleness and long-suffering. These gifts are spiritual fruit that come from the Holy Spirit. We must constantly do our best to continue to obey God's Word. We must always fight the battle of faith. It does not matter how many times we have failed, the Word of God promises victory to those who will endure until the end. Those who have a warrior mentality will do whatever it takes to obey God's instructions.

It is not only good for us to forgive, because the Word of God tells us so, however, when we release unforgiveness in our hearts, it can help us live a healthier lifestyle. Many become physically sick because of bitterness dwelling in their heart towards someone who hurt them. They never released that individual from their heart. Now they are captive to their own bitterness. The Holy Spirit is a sweet and gentle being. He is looking for a heart that He can rest and use that heart to demonstrate the power of His love. Because God is love, He will not tolerate His children to walk in hatred and hostility. Those traits are not of God but rather are come from the devil.

Whenever we disobey God's Word by not forgiving someone, we allow the enemy to have control over us, and as a result, he will keep us in captivity or in bondage. When we live our lives by *choosing* to keep a grateful heart toward those who hurt us, we prove to God that we are determined to walk in His love even when it does not feel good. We should never be the one to try to avenge anyone. God sometimes allows someone to hurt us simply to see if we are going to pass the test of forgiveness.

Forgiveness has played a big role in our Christian journey since the days of Jesus. One disciple asked Jesus how many times that he should forgive his brother or sister, and Jesus said, "seventy times seven times"(Matt.18:22). As we can see, we do not have any choice when it comes to forgiving those who have sinned against us. If we do not forgive our brothers and sisters, we will never be able to experience the complete peace of God in our lives. However, when we choose to walk in forgiveness, the very sweet presence of the Holy Spirit will always manifest in our lives. Consider the words of Jesus:

> *"You can only know a tree by it fruit. A good fruit will not produce bad fruit, and a bad fruit cannot produce good fruit. A tree is identified by the kind of fruit is produces. Figs never grow on thorn bushes or grapes on bramble bushes. A good person produces good deeds from a good heart, and an evil person produces evil deeds from an evil heart. Whatever is in your heart determines what you say," Jesus said* (Luke 6:43-45).

Whenever we hold someone hostage in our heart because of what they have done wrong, we are exercising an evil deed, which is against the will of God. Some people believe sexual sins are perhaps the greatest sins a believer can ever commit or fall into. However, when we are not walking in love or we are not willing to forgive others, the Bible says, the Father will not forgive you. (Matt.18:14) This shows how serious God takes His commandments in His Word. The Word of God has no partiality; we must make the necessary effort to obey everything from it. God loves His children very much, but He hates the fact that we are not walking in love reflecting His character. God called us to be the light of the world in every aspect of life.

There is no substitute for forgiveness. We cannot pay our way out of the disobedience of unforgiveness. It is a false premise to believe because you are a tithe paying member, that God will somehow overlook your unwillingness to forgive. What a false theology. Ministers sometimes forget the focus of the gospel was to receive Jesus as Lord and Savior and through His blood where there is forgiveness of sins. When we give our tithes to a local church, we must do it because we love God, and it is our responsibility as the body of Christ to support the church. If we truly love God, we will give Him back what He has given to us; therefore, I do not understand why we need to put pressure on people to give to God. I understand the gospel cannot be preached without financial support, but we need to educate believers about their responsibilities to support God's work, and to feed the people of God with good solid spiritual nourishment for their soul.

If we educate people, we won't need to put pressure on them or manipulate them about giving. After we have received Jesus as our Lord, we have to prove how much we are eager to serve Him by trusting Him. When we decide to obey Him, and to do whatever it takes to walk in forgiveness, we will truly show to the world that we are the children of God because our Father in heaven is expecting something great from His children. In other words, if we are going to distinguish ourselves from the world, we are going to have to learn to suffer things that do not make sense in their eyes. In order for us to do these things, we must constantly renew our minds with the Word and ask God to help us overcome anything that might seem impossible for us to conquer. If we do not forgive, it will be very difficult for us to sense the presence of God when we pray because of the unforgiveness we have carried in our hearts.

One time, I was very upset with my wife, and I did not resolve the situation with her before I went to bed. One day while I was praying, I could not sense God's presence. The Holy Spirit stopped me, and said, "If you do not forgive your wife, I will not hear anything you have to say." I thought she was wrong. Why should I forgive her, I told God. She was the one who did me wrong. Why won't you answer my prayer?

"How many times have you done me wrong, Tiery?" the Holy Spirit clearly asked me.

I could not continue to pray until I did what God had told me to do. When we hold unforgiveness toward an individual for a long time, God will withdraw His presence from us, because of sins that we have in our hearts. God will not answer our prayer, if we do not forgive, not only those whom we love, but even our enemies.

There was a time when I worked for a corporation and my supervisor was a very wicked man, who only cared about himself.   Everyone in the company complained about how he mistreated them. One day, because of a very simple misunderstanding between my supervisor and I, he sent me home for more than one week. When he called me into his office and told me to go home for that day, I lost my cool. I spoke to him in a way that was not godly at all. When I got home, I called some of my friends to pray with me that God would fire him from the company, because everyone in the corporation was overwhelmed by the way he was mistreating them. After I finished praying, God told me, "I cannot answer your prayer until you call your boss and tell him that you were sorry for the way you spoke to him the other day." At that point, I was too upset, and I did not want to apologize to my supervisor. Finally, I decided to swallow my pride. I called him and apologized. When I decided to forgive him for what he had done to me, I heard the voice of God say, *"Now I can work on your behalf."* Beloved, two weeks later, I found out that the man was fired from the company. He had been working for the company for more than seven years. I learned in that situation that God did not remove him from my way until I chose to release the unforgiveness that I had in my heart against him. It is very important for us to learn to forgive quickly so we do not allow the enemy to have control over our minds. When we hold unforgiveness in our hearts, we allow Satan to have access to go to the throne of God and accuse us before the Father.

When a Christian holds bitterness against a person on the inside of him or herself, it becomes very difficult for that person to live in peace. I was in a situation where I needed to forgive someone, but it was very difficult for me to do so, because I refused to forgive that individual. The enemy attacked my thinking. For some reason, I could not even sleep at night. One day, I went to church, the man of God was preaching about the necessity of having a forgiving heart. Instantly, God spoke to me. He said the reason why you cannot sleep at night is that you have held unforgiveness against someone who is close to you, and Satan is controlling your mind because of your disobedience. When the preacher was getting ready to finish his sermon, he made an altar call for anyone that needed to release unforgiveness in their hearts to come forward. I went to the altar and left all the hurts that I had carried in me for many years. Thus, I was no longer bound by any resentments or bitterness. I was indeed a free man.

Friends, the moment I confessed my sins and released all the people I held captive, my life was not the same. I was able to live in peace with the Holy Spirit. I was able to sleep at night, which I could not do before. Today, maybe you are experiencing something similar where you do not have peace at night, and the only thing you think about is what someone did to you. It is time for you to seek the presence of the Lord and to ask Him to grant you the strength to forgive, so you can experience His peace. A person who is truly a believer in Christ Jesus should be able to have peace in any given circumstance if that person is committing his or her time in prayer. It will not be an easy thing for anyone to forgive, but the Holy Spirit will supernaturally help us overcome those hurts and emotions, which we have experienced in the pass. Once we decide to let go of our bitterness, the enemy cannot go before God and condemn us anymore. Whenever a believer decides to walk in forgiveness, he or she will always defeat the enemy, because that individual is walking in the love of God, and the blessing of God will be upon that person's life.

Many have prayed for God to bless them, but they hold grudges toward an individual, yet they wonder why God has not answered their prayers. Satan desires to find sins in our lives, so he can hinder the blessing of God from flowing into our lives if we are not careful to confess those sins. God will not change His , because of our prideful hearts. Jesus is the Son of God, yet He suffered many disappointments and unfair treatment. However, He chose to forgive instead of avenging or holding grudges. Peter, who was one of His closest friends, had denied Him, but Jesus understood that we are weak and that we will make mistakes. Jesus had a special love for Peter, and He had confidence in Him. However, He knew that Peter would make the mistake of denying Him and turning away from Him. If someone hurts us to the point that we cannot forgive him or her, it is because we are afraid of trusting God to bring justice in the situation. We must obey God by being submissive to His plan for our lives and know that if He allowed something to happen to us, it is because He wanted us to learn from the situation. Then we can minister to someone else, who might face something even greater than what we went through.

God wants to see His children expand every day, but in order for that to happen, we must undergo things that are unpleasing to us. If we love God and understand His loving kindness toward us, we would obey Him as soon as He tells us to do something. We would not hold grudges against others and prevent ourselves from hearing the voice of our Heavenly Father. Sometimes, the only thing that keeps me from sinning as a Christian is not that I love my wife and I do, or fear that people will talk bad about me as a pastor, or that my congregation will leave the church I pastor... it is simply because I love God. More importantly, I do not want to disappoint Him. When we decide to serve God, we will suffer even greater trials than the unbelievers who have nothing to do with God. We must stay in communion with God and ask Him to speak to us.

When we say that we love God, we must put actions in our words, because love is a commitment that must be fulfilled by every Christian. When we say that we love God, it is proven by our action. The Bible says, *"For God so loved the world that He gave his only Son, so that everyone who believes in Him will not perish but have eternal life,"* (John 3:16). God loved us so much that He proved himself to humanity by giving His only Son to die in our place. Therefore, if we say that we love God, we must prove it not only with our words but also by our actions. God would never ask us to forgive someone, if He did not recognize that we have the ability to do so. His desires are for us to keep a good heart, so we can live in peace with one another. God loves each one of His children the same. This is the reason why He loves to see us walking in love with one and other.

If we become intimate with God by being in His presence through prayer and worship, it will be easier for us to see the manifestation of His love in our lives. As a result, our hearts will be very sensitive to the things of God. If someone hurts us, it will not affect us emotionally because we have spent our times in the presence of God. Being in the presence of God on a daily basis will kill our natural flesh, and it will help us in controlling our emotions. Christians, who are easily hurt emotionally, are believers who have not yet developed a level of maturity in their relationship with God. As we begin to spend our time communicating with God, people will begin to see the character of God in our expressions. If we do not feed ourselves with spiritual nourishments, we will never be able to implement any spiritual task, which God has assigned us to accomplish. As believers, we should be able to manage our spiritual lives and do whatever it takes to follow the counsel of the Holy Spirit whenever He brings something to our attentions. We have to do the best we can to obey Him as quickly as possible. Sometimes, it could be very difficult to forgive an individual, while the negative memories are constantly haunting our minds.

From my experiences, whenever I experienced a painful situation and those bad memories kept coming back into my mind, I asked God to purify my thinking with His. The truth is, even after we have decided to forgive an individual, who has done us wrong, the emotions can sometimes still want to rise in our brains. However, we have to make a decision that we will not allow those emotions to keep us bound and seek to keep our mind on Christ. It could be a big challenge for us to let go of certain things, but God will not tolerate a believer who has purposely made up his/her mind to hold an individual captive in his/her heart and who never prays to ask God to help him or her to forgive that person. We have to do the best we can, so we do not dwell on our past. When all those thoughts keep coming back and forth in our minds, we need to know that it is nothing but a trick from Satan.

Our God is a loving and patient Father. He wants the willingness from His children to obey Him and to please Him. If our desires are only to do the will of God, what people said or did to us will not affect our lives. Our focus should be only about fulfilling the plan of God and the function of the Kingdom of heaven. Therefore, we will not allow Satan to bring any distraction on our paths that God has preordained for us. We are going to run the race no matter what we have to face in our journey. I will sing the tender mercies of the Lord forever! Young and old will hear that your faithfulness is as enduring as the heavens. (Psalm 89: 1-2) Choose to forgive. Choose life!

CHAPTER 8
TRUSTING GOD

We are almost there... Every chapter is saturated with this reoccurring idea. As we pray and apply God's Word, we can choose life. Not just any life, but you can choose the abundant life. We cannot fathom such a life without trusting God. Trusting God is a decision believers have to make on their own. The truth of the matter is learning to trust God is a process. Trusting in God is required for believers to use their faith day by day and invite the Holy Spirit to instruct them how to develop that trust in God. When we were unbelievers, we used to do everything based on our carnal mindsets. Therefore, we made decisions based our intellect and human wisdom. We used to operate based on our senses and our intuition. God now expects us to think and make decisions leaning on the wisdom of His Son, Jesus Christ. So how do we put our complete trust in Him? Maybe right now you are reading this book, and you are asking yourself, how can you develop trust in God? If you have perhaps been a believer for many years, but you never really trusted God with your entire life, I am going to tell you how to trust God completely.

Let's first define what it means to trust God. Trusting God is to give Him control with our lives; to give Him access to do whatever He wishes to do in us. In order for us to trust God, we are going to have to develop a daily relationship with Him by inviting Him into every aspect of our lives and therefore ask Him to be a part of our daily activities.

CHILDLIKE FAITH

Children are fascinating. They live life with such a carefree spirit. They have no worries or fears. They just believe, wholeheartedly; God desires that same spirit from us in our faith walk with Him. Just believe.

When we become as little children, we prove to God that we humbly want to live for Him by renouncing our ways of thinking in order to allow His will to be fulfilled in our lives. The Bible mentions that some children were brought to Jesus, so He could lay His hands on them and pray for them. The disciples told them not to bother Him. But Jesus said, *"Let the children come to me. Do not stop them! For the Kingdom of Heaven belongs to such as these"* (Matthew 19:13-14). This illustration represents how the body of Christ needs to put their trust in God, and to be submissive to the way of the kingdom of God.

Let's start at the beginning of our faith. Jesus said, *"Unless one is born again, you cannot see the Kingdom of God,"* (John 3: 3). The very first step anyone must take in order for one to enter in His Kingdom, one must be born of water and of the Spirit. After we have received the Spirit of God, we will begin to develop confidence in His Word as we begin to devote ourselves in prayer and reading His Word. Once we begin to cultivate our relationships with God, it will be very easy for us to trust Him more on a personal level.

When we come in the kingdom of God, our spirits need to be renewed by the Holy Spirit in order that we may walk agreement with His plan for our future. Trusting God will require believers to spend time in His Word, meditating and allowing God to have direct access in our lives. The Holy Spirit who knows all things will begin to lead us in the direction that our Father has intended for us to go. God has a great plan for each of His children and all we have to do is obey. Unfortunately, God's path is not problem free. It is in the face of difficulty that we often divert from the plan of God.

STANDING ON THE WORD

T.V. Shows… Popular Magazines… Reality Specials… Breaking News!!! We are constantly exposed to a very secular worldview. We are not only exposed to it but often influenced by it. We cannot put our trust in God while operating on world's standards. God gave His Word to believers to equip us and inform us in our everyday living. The Bible should be the only book that God's people use to lay their foundation as opposed to education, wealth, or the people with whom we associate. God gave us His Word to lead us into the path that He wants us to follow in life. God will never force anyone to serve Him nor do His will. This is something that we must decide to do on our own. God will give us the faith to trust His Word, however ... we must walk out that faith in how we live.

Some people will give more value to something that they have heard on television than what the Bible says. We must always remember the Word of God is the only truth that we must live by. It should be the only thing to govern our lives. Satan wants to contradict the Word by using entertainment to lead the people of God astray. The enemy is very busy. Therefore, the body of Christ needs to be busier. We cannot serve God nor do the things of God without invoking the help of the Holy Spirit, so He can continue to help us operate in the Spirit and understand the things that come from the Spirit. This is why we need to engage ourselves in prayer, and to make prayer our lifestyle. When we have a prayerful life, we allow the Holy Spirit to take control of our lives, and He will lead us in the direction that He wishes for us to take. God will not lead our lives if we do not allow Him. Unless we decide to come into agreement with the Spirit of God and admit to ourselves that we are nothing without Him, He will never be able to entrust us with His plan.

Not only can God's Word guide us, it gives us examples of people who have completed the task before us. God's Word provides us with a plethora of witnesses such as Abraham, Moses and David. These great men of God trusted God with everything. God's Word should be the very first thing believers run to whenever we find ourselves in a situation, which might seem difficult for us to bear. The Word of God helps us to understand that we are not alone. Trusting in God's Word is the only thing that helps me overcome many situations in my life. As a pastor, I often minister to the people in my church. I encourage them to put their complete faith and trust in God's Word. I admonish them that God will never fail them. No matter what is going on, God is always in control.

When we do not understand our situations and circumstances of life, we need to encourage ourselves in the Word of God, because our Heavenly Father cannot lie. If He made a promise to His children, He will make sure that the promise comes to pass.

GIVE US THIS DAY...

We must nurture our soul constantly by listening to the teaching of God's Word day and night and usher in His Holy presence at all times. In exchange, the Holy Spirit will help us strengthen our faith in Him. There was man in the Bible that was born blind.

The disciples asked Jesus, "Teacher, why was this man born blind? Was it as result of his own sins or those of his parents?" "It was not because of his or his parents' sins. He was born blind so the power of God could be seen in him." All of us must carry out the task assigned to us by the one who sent us because there is little time left before the night falls and all work comes to an end. But while I am still here in the

world, I am the light of the world," said Jesus
(John 9: 2-5).

Many times in life, we've found ourselves in
situations, which we do not understand. Sometimes,
people will even go as far as criticizing us, because they
do not understand the plans of God for our lives.
However, in regard of the blind man, I do not believe
the disciples were the only ones who were convinced
that the beggar must have done something wrong or his
parents. I assume many people had the same question in
mind. Have you ever found yourself in situations in
which you have no control over? God could be the One
who has brought the dilemmas into your life, so He
could display His glory through you. People begin to
talk very horrifically about your situation because they
do not understand what God is doing in your life.

God knows each of our needs. He expects His
children to depend on Him for whatever necessities we
might have. God yearns for us to put His Kingdom first,
and to prioritize the works of the Kingdoms. Then He
will give us everything we need from day to day.
Consider this passage.

> *"So don't worry about having enough food or*
> *drink or clothing. Why be like the pagans who*
> *are so deeply concerned about these things?*
> *Your heavenly Father already knows all your*
> *needs, and He will give you all you need from*
> *day to day if you live for Him and make the*
> *Kingdom of God your primary concern. So do*

not worry about tomorrow, for tomorrow will bring its own worries. Today's trouble is enough for today." (Matthew 6:31-34)

God is the maker of the universe; He knows the beginning and the end. Let us not allow anything or anyone to keep us away from the blessing of God for our lives. We have to remember that we have an enemy who is always trying to deceive the children of God by bringing doubts and distractions into our minds. Satan also has his own agents on the earth. His agents are the people who allow the enemy to control their minds. The Word teaches you that "greater is He that is in you than he who is in the world" (I John 4:4). We must learn to walk in that authority in our homes, on our jobs and in our community... trusting the God in us. If you are a Christian, and someone is harassing you on the job for no reason, that individual is being controlled by an evil spirit. Satan has assigned that person against you. In a situation like this, you must know how to pray and command that evil spirit to come out of the individual, and then you will see that person will no longer harass you. Otherwise, your prayer will not be effective. God's Word should be the very first thing believers run to whenever we find ourselves in a situation, which might seem difficult for us to bear. The Word of God helps us to understand that we are not alone. Trusting in God's Word is the only thing, which helps me overcome many situations in my life. Many times as a pastor, I ministered to the people in my church. I encouraged them to put their complete faith and trust in God's Word and that God will never fail them. No matter what is going on, God is always in control.

It takes courage and humility to do the will of God. Sometimes, walking in the plan of God for our lives can be a very lonely journey. People probably thought Abram was fanatical, because he had everything he needed. He was living in the same land with his close relatives, and he had so much wealth. He was living the perfect life. One day, God came and took him out of his comfortable place. I assume even his family probably disagreed with him about leaving his current land to go to a place where Abram would be a stranger in the land. What I like the most about this story is that the blessing was prearranged, not only for him but also for everyone who would obey God. God was looking for someone who was willing to obey Him and trust in Him, and as a result, the whole world would benefit from his obedience. God told Abram,

> *Leave your country, your relatives, and your father's house, and go to the land that I will show you. I will cause you to become the father of a great nation. I will bless you and make you famous, and I will make you a blessing to others. I bless those who bless you and curse those who curse you. All the families of the earth will be blessed through you* (Genesis 12:1-3).

It takes a lot of faith for Abram to do something like this. Abram was already wealthy with many possessions. However, he wasn't thinking about how God was going to bring it to pass. When the Lord asked him to leave his native country, he had to trust Him. Sometimes, in order for us to put our complete trust in God, we must be willing to lose something or someone that we may love dearly. Whenever God asks His people to give up something, it is because He wants to see if we love Him more than what He gave to us.

Some people tend to love their possessions more than they love God. God will never come in second position in our lives. We must put Him first in everything we do. Nothing is more important than obeying Him. We should never wait when we face difficulties to get on our knees before God. When we say that we truly love God, we should always want to have the desire to spend time with Him. If we really love God, we will enjoy being in His presence. God is an awesome Father to His children. Before we were yet born, God already set a great future for our lives. No one can stop us from achieving the plans of God for our lives. Not even the devil has the power to hinder us from carrying out the plan of God. The only people who have the power to stop us from executing His plan for our lives are ourselves through unbelief. Many believers have trusted the world's perspectives more than they trust God.

Nothing moves our Lord Jesus Christ more than when He can truly see that His children put their complete faith in Him in everything they do. The Bible says, *"Therefore, since we have been made right with*

God by faith, we have peace with God because of what Jesus Christ our Lord has done for us. Because of our faith, Christ has brought us into this place of highest privilege, where we now stand, and we confidently and joyfully look forward to sharing God's glory," (Roman 5:1-2).

Maybe right now you are reading this book, and you are asking yourself, how can you develop trust in God? If you have perhaps been a believer for many years, but you never really trusted God with your entire life, I am going to tell you how to trust God completely. We must ask ourselves how we do we trust. Trusting God is to give Him control of our lives; to give Him access to do whatever He wishes to do in us. Let's say that you have a child, who has been sick for a very long time, and you ask God to heal that child, but God has not answered your prayers; if you really trust God even if He has not healed your child, you still have to trust Him. Moreover, you should never stop praying nor stop believing in Him. After we have received the Spirit of God, we will begin to develop confidence in Him as we begin to devote ourselves in prayer and reading His Word.

When we decide to follow Christ, we must set our minds and therefore prepare ourselves to endure things that don't have anything to do with us directly. Jesus was the Son of God, and God allowed Him to go through sufferings and disappointments that were not 'for' Him. Jesus chose to let go of His will, so the will of the Father can be carried out into the world. He went through the most painful situation, so He could bring glory to His Father.   The truth is nothing was more essential for Jesus than to see the will of His Father fulfilled.

Consider the prophets. God utilized many prophets in the Bible, so He could illustrate His points to the children of Israel.   Let us take an example from the prophet Hosea. The Bible says when the Lord began speaking to Israel through the prophet Hosea, He said to him, *"Go and marry a prostitute, so some of her children will be born from other men. This will illustrate the way my people have been so untrue to me; they openly commit adultery against the Lord by worshipping other gods"* (Hosea 1:2). God wanted to demonstrate the unfaithfulness of the children of Israel. Therefore, Hosea, a man of God, had to go through all these trials so God could make the illustration that He wanted to make. Can you imagine how many religious friends Hosea lost because of the decision to obey God? I believe even family members turned away from him, as they believed Hosea's decision was unwise. Perhaps they were thinking that Hosea had a demonic spirit in him for marrying a prostitute.

When we go through something similar to what Hosea went through, let it be an opportunity for us to bring glory to God. We found in the scriptures many prophets, men of God, who went through some terrible situations. God fashioned them, so He could illustrate His point to others. If God allows us to face troubles, it is because He trusts us, so we can demonstrate His glory to the world. If we had never experienced any sickness in our body, how would we know that God is a healer, or if we had never encountered persecutions and trials, how would we know that our Father is able to deliver us from our troubles?

Whenever we find ourselves in isolation, and people do not understand our position, we have to remain faithful and know that God is doing something new in us. Every time God is getting ready to bless His people, He will use an impossible situation. Throughout the scriptures, we can see how many times God used pains and sufferings to bring glory to Himself. In the book of Genesis chapters 37-47, we read the story of Joseph; how God gave him a dream about his future, and how his family would bow before him, and God would make him a very prominent man in Egypt. Joseph endured many unfair treatments, many pains and disappointments before the glory of God was significantly manifested in his life. He was sold into slavery. He worked for many years in Potiphar's house, the captain of palace guard, and lastly, he was imprisoned.

We want to share the glory of God, but we are not willing to pick up our cross and go through the process. Before his dream finally came to pass, Joseph was most likely thinking that God had forsaken him after thirteen years of trials and tribulations. We need to learn how to enjoy ourselves, while we are going through the process. The mistake we make is we stop living our lives and quit enjoying life because we feel like that

God is taking too long to answer our prayers. Friends, God know when everything is going to take place. Therefore, our prayers and our obedience toward God cannot force Him to do something before its appointed time. We should continue to stay faithful in whatever task that He has placed us and assigned us to accomplish, never letting people or our circumstances cause us to abort the plans of God for our lives.

When we face dilemmas in our lives, what we must do is to keep our eyes focused on God, and expect Him to bring us out of the problem. God will not deliver us if we do not believe that He has the power to do so. It requires faith and perseverance in Him for us to see the power of God manifests in our lives. These trials are only to test your faith, to show that it is strong and pure. It is being tested as fire tests and purifies gold and your faith is far more precious to God than mere gold. So if your faith remains strong after being tried by fiery trails, it will bring you much praise and honor on the day when Jesus Christ is revealed to the whole world (1 Peter1:7).

When we go through quandary, God wants to see us develop faith and character, so we can completely trust in His power. Many times the reason why people cannot see the glory of God come into manifestation is that they have not yet entirely surrendered themselves to God. If we face oppositions in life, and if we had the ability to control the situations, we would not need God to help us overcome the situation; we would have confidence in ourselves to do it on our own. On the other hand, if we let the Lord know that without Him, we cannot do anything. If we humble ourselves before Him and depend only on His capability to bring us out, we will therefore allow Him to work on our behalf.

God does not need to use our strengths nor our aptitudes to perform anything, or to bring anything into realization. However, the only thing He requires from us is our faith. Our faith is what will move God the most, not our money or even our worship. When we prove to Him that we trust His Word, God will make the impossible become possible. God will answer our prayers when we truly trust His Word and put His Word into application. God gave us His Word, so we could find the right way to live according to His principles. Let's choose to trust Him!

CHAPTER 9
THE LOVE OF GOD

I could not close this book without talking about the love of God. There is no abundant life to live if God had not loved us. Christians have lived their lives without understanding the kind of love that God has for them. Some people think that they can earn God's love by their works, and some believe that they can pay a price to earn God's love. God's love is not something that the human mind can fully understand. Even the angels could not understand why God loves His creation so much. God made men in His own image. God loves us so much that He made us men in His own likeness. God's love is unconditional. God will always love His children no matter what we have done. He will never stop loving us. Write this on the tablet of your heart. God loves me.

LOVING US PASS SIN

> *Now the serpent was the shrewdest of all the creatures the Lord God had made. Really? He asks the woman. Did God really say you must not eat any of the fruit in the garden? Of course we may eat it, the woman told him. It's only the*

fruit from the tree at the center of the garden that we are not allowed to eat. God says we must not eat or even touch it, or we will die. You will not die the serpent hissed. God knows that your eye will be opened when you eat it. You will become just like God, knowing everything, both good and evil. The woman was convinced. The fruit looked so fresh and delicious, and it would make her so wise! Therefore, she ate some of the fruit. She also gave some to her husband, who was with her. Then he ate it, too. (Gen. 3:1-6)

When Satan realized how much God cared for humanity, he thought that he was going to disappoint God. What Satan did not understand was that God's love would always triumph over anything. God had a second plan for the sins of humanity. God's love was greater than man's failure. He brought men back into relationship with Him by His Son Jesus whom He gave to die in our place, so we can once more have eternal life. Did you know that if Jesus had not come and died for us, we would be dead and separated from the presence of God eternally? In addition, Satan would have become our master. We would not have the ability to defeat him. The fact that Jesus died on the cross for our sins not only brings us back to the Father, He also redeemed us, and gave us all the power to destroy Satan's works. Because of the shared blood of Jesus Christ, now we have the power over sins, and over any wicked spirits that have come against the people of God. Because of the blood that Jesus had shed for us on

Calvary, we can now tell the devil to get under our feet, and he will. This would be a good place to pause and just say, "Thank you Jesus!"

Whenever I find myself in a situation where I feel a little discouraged, I've learned to remind myself about the love that Christ has for me. For I know because of His love for me, He will change my circumstances. God thinks about us just as a Father thinks about his children's future. He always has us in mind, and He has a great plan for His children. His love saved us from sins and redeemed us from all unrighteousness, so we can have a relationship with Him. Since the beginning of time, God's intention was to see humanity enjoy life and everything that He made available to us. He never wanted to see His people suffer or lack any good thing. Suffering and lack exist because of Adam and Eve's disobedience. However, we should thank God for His Son Jesus Christ, who gave us back the power to live our lives in the over flow. The salvation of Jesus Christ is a gift; we don't have to work for it. All we have to do is to accept it. However, when it comes for us to receive the blessing of God, we have to do our parts in order for us to experience His blessing. God already made provision for His children, but all we have to do is to walk in His absolute will.

When we rest in the love of God, we will feel that there is a sense of reliance and security in His love for us. God wants to be involved in our daily activities, so He can protect us and show us the proper path to follow for our future. God's love brings honor to His Son

Jesus. When we know how much our heavenly Father loves us, we will no longer concern ourselves about the things of this world that do not have any significance. When we learn to walk in the love of God for our lives, we will begin to develop great spiritual fruits, and people will begin to identify the light of Christ in us. We need to emulate our Lord Jesus Christ in everything we do and by the way, we live our lives. The love of God will take us to places that money could not. The Psalmist said, *"Your unfailing love will last forever. Your faithfulness is as enduring as the heavens."* (Psalm 89:2). Nothing in this world can compare with God's love for His children. Even when we miss the mark, God will correct us in love for our mistakes or failures. He has so much love for us, so whenever we find ourselves in a situation where there is no way out, we can cry out to Him, and He will rescue us from that situation.

If it appears that we face something, which is too overwhelming to bear, we need to remember that God is a loving Father, who loves and cares for His children, so He will never allow us to be in a situation, which is too difficult to bear. The thing is when we face a terrible circumstance, we tend to focus on the setback instead of focusing on the love that God has for us. Consequently, Satan who is the father of deception brings confusion in our minds and makes us forget all the promises that God gave us in His. God promises us that He will never leave us nor forsake us, so if we continuously remember those promises that He made to us, no trials or conditions will be able to take us away from His love.

We need to stay alert and be aware of the deception of the devil. Satan doesn't want believers to recognize how much God cares for them. This is why when we experience a tragic situation, the first question Satan will bring before us is "If God really loved you, why did He let something like that happen to you or to your loved ones?" Many people who have lost loved ones prematurely have turned away from God and stopped serving Him. For instance, they might blame God for accidental deaths or the loved ones who died because of sickness but prayed and believed that God would heal them. We do not serve our heavenly Father based on what He can do for us; we serve Him for who He is. Abraham was a man who loved God and walked with God. Nevertheless, God tested His faith to see if Abraham was willing to sacrifice His only son, whom he loved dearly. When we truly love the Lord with all our hearts, minds and souls, nothing on earth will be more important for us than to please Him.

When someone is truly in love with another individual, he will do anything to please the individual, whom he or she is in love with, because that person wants to maintain a healthy relationship with the other. Likewise, if we say we love God, we ought to please Him. Therefore, we will do our best to continue to maintain a passionate relationship with Him, not only by obeying His , but also by spending most of our time in His presence, so we can know His intentions and understand His purposes. The love of God will bring believers out of bondage and set us free from yokes or captivities that we might struggle with for many years. One touch from our Lord will transform everything in our lives. God's love is a shelter for His children, so if we need a place to rest ourselves, God is our refuge. If we look at His creations, we will see God's affection for humanity.

God gives everyone the ability, gifts and talents to serve Him. We need to walk in the love of God and start loving our brothers and sisters, so the wisdom of God will begin to develop strongly in us. The Holy Spirit, who is the distributor of the gifts, will begin to empower us, so we can have success in whatever task we'll perform for the Kingdom. If believers are not living in peace, it is because the love of God has not yet rooted in the inside of those people and they do not yet have a revelation of Jesus as the Prince of Peace. If we had put our complete hope in Him and started using those abilities that God had invested in us, we would be able to walk in perfect peace at all times.

Every time we find ourselves in a situation, which might cause us not to trust God, we need to always remember how much God loves us. Besides, His love will over power any trials or tribulations we can encounter. When we learn to operate in the love of God, the enemy will tremble in our presence, so let us do our best to walk in love, so we can continue to bring light into this dark world. We are the light of the world. Let us shine by displaying the character of God in everything we do. When the world sees that we have joy, peace, prosperity and kindness, they will desire Christ. Now let us always remember how much our heavenly Father loves His children. Don't take God's love for granted.

> *"And I am convinced that nothing can ever separate us from His love. Death can't, and life can't. The angels can't, and the demons can't. Our fears for today, our worries about tomorrow, and even the powers of hell can't keep God's love away. Whether high above the sky or in the deepest ocean, nothing in all creation will ever be able to separate us from the love of God that is revealed in Christ Jesus our Lord."* (Romans 8:38-39)

CHAPTER 10
THE PRIVILEGE OF HOLINESS

God chose His children to be a holy nation, not because we were holy from the beginning, but because of what His Son Jesus Christ did on Calvary. Many have wrongly portrayed holiness. Holiness is to be in one mind with God. We were separated from God, but Jesus came on earth and adopted us, so He could bring us into the family of God. When we accepted Christ as our Lord and Savior, we have become the children of God. Therefore, we inherit holiness by the ransom Jesus Christ had paid for our sins.

> *"For God knew his people in advance, and He chose them to become like His Son so that He would be the firstborn with many brothers and sisters. And having chosen them, He called them to come to Him. And gave them right standing with Himself, and He promises them His glory.* (Romans 8:29-30)"

What we must know as believers how to live a holy life. First, we must understand that holiness is a lifestyle. I would like to focus on the steps necessary that we need to take as Christians in order for us to walk in holiness with God. Just because we have been made right with God by the shaded blood of Jesus Christ, it does not mean that we can live any kind of way we want. We must do our part if we want to continue to walk in His righteousness. We must not take the grace of God for granted. Jesus lived a lifestyle on earth, which was very pleasing to His Father. If we have the mind of Christ, and His Spirit living within in us, we should triumph over the struggle within to do the will of God.

When we desire only the things of the Spirit, our bodies, too, will desire to do the things of the Spirit. However, if we only feed our minds with the things of the world, we will begin to produce the things of the world. What you feed grows, and what you don't feed dies. The reality is if we are afraid to separate ourselves from the affair of this world, we will never be able to fully live a lifestyle that pleases God. Sometimes we have to deny people in order for us to live in holiness. To walk in holiness, it will take effort and discipline. In other words, we have to discipline our flesh to obey the Word of God even when we do not feel like it. Holiness is to love the things of God and to renounce the things of the world.

Holiness is not self-attained. Some people believe that they are religious by observing rules and regulations. The truth is…we have been made righteous by the grace of God. Some people believe that they can earn salvation through their works and good deeds. We can please God only by faith. We need to keep reminding ourselves on a day-to-day basis regarding how we can live a daily life that is pleasing to our Heavenly Father. When we wake up in the morning, we need to think about how we can improve ourselves, and what can we do to enhance the Kingdom of God, because we are God's ambassadors. Our heavenly Father will not perform anything on earth unless He revealed it to His ambassadors. *"The Sovereign Lord does nothing without revealing to His prophets"* (Amos 3:7). Therefore, we must continue to make ourselves available, so God can continue to reveal to us the things that He wants to clear on the earth.

If believers would truly walk in holiness, we would be able to hear the voice of our Lord Jesus at all time. God chose us to be holy just as Christ is Holy. Thus, it is imperative that the body of Christ be a holy nation. God did not choose us, because we were better than the world. He chose us because we have received His Son as our Lord and savior. Jesus said that anyone who decides to be my disciple must carry his cross and follow me. When a believer makes a decision to serve God with all of his or her heart and mind, he/she will suffer trials and persecution. We will need the help of the comforter, who is the Holy Spirit, so He can help us live a holy lifestyle in God. Therefore, we will be able to walk in the perfect will of God. The Holy Spirit gives us the strength we need to conquer any obstacle, which we could not overcome with our natural strength.

The Holy Spirit also helps us to live a sanctified life. When we allow Him to be the one to direct our lives in every aspect, He gives us the potency necessary, so we can live a holy life. It is clear that without the help of the Holy Spirit, we are only fooling ourselves. The Holy Spirit gives us the ability to consecrate our lives, so we can develop a prayerful lifestyle by inviting God in everything we do, and to do our best to follow His commandments even when no one is looking at us. I assume that if we really want to live for God, we will not wait for when people are watching us to do what is right. I heard it said that character is what you do when no one is looking. God honors His children best when we have the opportunity to do wrong, but instead, we decide to obey His Word. When a believer puts the Word of God first, that individual proves that he/she has a profound relationship with God. However, if someone is not willing to deepen his or her relationship with our Lord Jesus, that person will not have the stability to trust God's Word. We cannot have a close relationship with Him until we decide to get to know Him. We must invest the time to know a holy God that we might live a holy life.

We have to discipline ourselves if we are going to walk a victorious life in God. It is pivotal that the body of Christ never stops walking in holiness. We need to ask Him to give us the spirit of wisdom, so we can understand how to operate in His holiness. When we walk in the holiness of God, we prove that we are children of God and the reflection of His Son, Jesus the Messiah. The kinds of clothes that we wear are not going to differentiate that we are holy citizens of God's kingdom. What will distinguish us is when we bring the very nature of our heavenly Father on the earth by walking in love with one another. Once the world can see the everlasting love, which God has for them through us believers, we will influence their lives with the good news of Jesus Christ.

CLOSING THOUGHTS:

My final words for everyone: If God has talked to you while reading this book, do the best you can to apply what you have learned, because the Holy Spirit has inspired me to write this book. If you make a decision that you are going to apply whatever you have learned in this text, I assure you, by the power of the Holy Spirit, that your life will never be the same. Enjoy grace… enjoy abundant living!

ABOUT THE AUTHOR
TIERY PHANOR

Tiery Phanor was originally born in Haiti and moved to
Miami in 1996. After moving to the U.S. his faith was
both tested and strengthened by overcoming various
trials. Tiery Phanor found a passion to preach the
gospel, as a result, pursued a degree in theology at the
University of Fort Lauderdale. He has also worked and
served at World Changers Church International, under
Dr. Creflo Dollar, for over two years and served various
other ministries. He eventually became the Senior
Pastor of Revelation of Church in Miami, Florida.
Pastor Phanor is also the founder of Covenant People
Incorporated, which produces Christian products, such
as baby clothing, kids clothing, women's clothing and
printed materials. He also possesses various talents as a
singer, songwriter, and author.
Tiery Phanor has two beautiful children Kayann J
Phanor and Arthur J Phanor, and a lovely wife Tonia.
Tonia Phanor, previously Tonia East, is also an

accomplished inspirational author, speaker, and teacher. Tiery and Tonia Phanor are both very committed to impacting people's life for Christ through books, ministry, and kingdom businesses. To make contact or to order products, go to www.covenantpeople.net or www.tieryphanor.com.

30043000R00078

Made in the USA
Charleston, SC
03 June 2014